A YEOMAN
FARMER'S SON

A YEOMAN FARMER'S SON

A Leicestershire Childhood

H. St G. Cramp

JOHN MURRAY

© H. St G. Cramp 1985

First published 1985
by John Murray (Publishers) Ltd
50 Albemarle Street, London WIX 4BD

Typeset by Richard Clay (The Chaucer Press) Ltd
Printed and bound in Great Britain
by The Pitman Press, Bath

British Library CIP Data
Cramp, Harold St G.
A yeoman farmer's son: a Leicestershire childhood.
1. Villages—England—Leicestershire—History
—20th century 2. Leicestershire—Social
life and customs
I. Title
942.5'4082   DA670.L5
ISBN 0-7195-4199-9

Contents

List of Illustrations

*To the Family Cramp
and the Folk of Tur Langton
who kept their feet on the ground
and their heads in the air.
Also to Berenice, my wife,
for practical support and
constant encouragement
in my endeavours.*

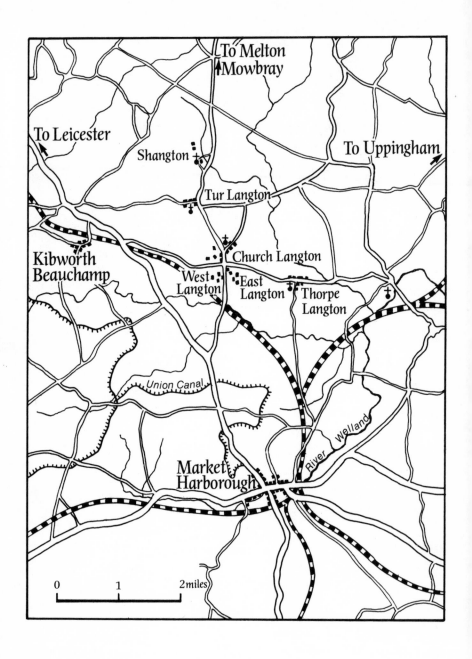

To Melton
Mowbray

To Leicester

To Uppingham

Shangton

Tur Langton

Kibworth
Beauchamp

Church Langton

West
Langton

East
Langton

Thorpe
Langton

Union Canal

River Welland

Market
Harborough

0   1   2 miles

The Place
Where I Was Born

WHEN I WAS YOUNG, Langton lay at the centre of
the world, and the centre of Langton was my home.
Heaven was somewhere in our kitchen and quite often in
the pantry. Sometimes when I was very tired, it moved
upstairs to a feather bed and there remained to greet me
in the morning. I have known it to be in the dog's kennel
when I curled up with him and slept unknown to the
world. I found it once in a dragonfly's wing floating on a
pond and I have seen it in the moon's reflection in that
same place.

Yet Langton lays no claim to beauty: we have few
thatched cottages, no market cross or mediaeval church.
The straight main street climbs gently uphill, to be crossed
at the top by another, making a letter 'T'. The houses
follow the line of the rough metalled road; so does the
footpath flanked by a granite kerb. There is no view to
admire and at the 'T' junction, wooden fingers point
clear alternatives. So to dally is to stand exposed and invite
suspicion from disembodied heads that loll round the
doors of labourers' cottages. Should you use the footpath,
have a care for your feet; cows use it in preference to the
potholed road.

Houses of substantial yeoman farmers hide behind
limetrees and laurel. Rutted drives pierce the spaces
between them, ending in barn, byre and midden, and the
whole village smells of farm. A few grander homes of
gentleman farmers rise up three-storied from islands of
green; in summer croquet balls clack behind box hedges
and hoarse-throated guinea fowl guard the drive. The
labourers live in redbrick warrens, all doors and passages.

The women folk, like restless rabbits, pop in and out, to nibble at one another's lives, to chitter-chatter, borrow and sometimes row. Lost in a field at the bottom of the village, a stonebuilt manor house sighs for the past. But the elms in the drive are blasted and cows splash in the mediaeval moat.

Tur Langton, the scene of my story, is one of five similarly named villages, a sort of constellation of Langtons: East, West, Church, Thorpe—and Tur. Though recorded in Domesday Book their history has been singularly uneventful. The plough, the ox, the cow, the labourer and the farmer have dominated this quiet corner of east Leicestershire.

The Romans moving up the Gartree Road, the *Via Devana*, three miles distant ignored us. But the Saxons penetrating up the Welland valley recognised the merits of our soil and settled. The very name 'Lang-ton' suggests long straggling Saxon 'tons' or townships which indeed we are. Domesday Book lists our ploughland and waste. Our history is under our feet: ridge and furrow tell the tale. But the heavy clay land has increasingly been laid to grass, and the Hereford bullock loved by my father now grazes where the ox once leaned into the yoke. If we have an industry it is hunting, for the Fernie Hunt still chase the fox over lush meadows between scattered coverts.

Just occasionally we were touched by great men or events. Out of West Langton came Walter de Langton, Lord Treasurer of King Edward I. In the sixteenth century the Pope sent the quaintly named Polydore Vergil from Rome to be rector of Church Langton. In 1645 legend says Charles I paused briefly at Tur Langton after his defeat at Naseby. Here, at a chalybeate spring still named King Charles's Well he is said to have watered his horse. But local folk remember the spring better for its curative powers, especially for sore eyes. Few other great names have touched us. Like most English villagers we lived uncomplicated lives despite wars, revolutions and political turmoil. Such are the brief annals of my birthplace though my childhood visions had a very different horizon.

WE ONCE had three public houses, at the bottom, middle and top of the village respectively. The Chequers, The Crown and The Bull's Head catered for a community of three hundred. But one hundred souls vanished and The Chequers closed its doors. The other two pubs survived on the thirst of some thirty regulars, but the owners were driven to piecework for farmers, to make ends meet. Outwardly little distinguished the two pubs; majestic inn signs gave no hint of the spartan interiors. Yet the village folk saw fine distinctions, and not only in the ale. Which one lit its fires early, so that a man could relax as he drank? Was carpet under your feet in the Snug at The Bull worth an extra farthing a pint? Did you prefer to stand your ale on upturned barrels, or on tables that waltzed on a redbrick floor? And how did you rate a covered urinal against a plain zinc sheet set at an angle to a pigsty? Should you move up the road where a 'good drop' was fresh on tap or stay where you were with beer 'cloudy as hosspiss' because, being Friday, a well covered barmaid helped to serve? Did you like bright copper spittoons, or prefer to spit into the sawdust, and watch the globules snowball towards the open fire? And what was devil-among-the-tailors compared with a full-sized skittle alley, where chewing gum was needed to keep the skittles vertical? On such niceties as these, loyalties swung back and forth, but Crown and Bull's Head both stayed in business.

Over the width of the village street, the Church stared the Crown Inn full in the face. But the latter was dispensing comfort to the parishioners long before the advent of its redbrick rival, built in 1866 in Early English style by an eccentric parson. Since Sunday matins coincided with opening time, church and pub competed on equal terms.

Nor was it easy on Sunday morning to distinguish their respective clientele. All were dressed in their Sunday best, all used the only footpath on the same side of the road as the church. Not till the very last minute did the sheep and the goats divide. There were those with tender consciences who moved to the very brink of heaven's gate, only to vanish with sudden sidestep into the opposing camp. To further confound the onlooker, the verger might quickly wet his whistle before hastening to the parson's business. The bellringer in his open porch stood in the very eye of the storm, sorely tempted by the sight of The Crown Inn sign. He had been known to desert his post as the last clang sounded and cross the great divide. But the pints that tasted best, said the faithful few, were those drunk with a clear conscience after doing the Lord's bidding.

At the top of the street, a rival scene was enacted, for there The Bull's Head sign nodded in the wind. Its gaudy blazon held hidden promise of four-x ale which would gladden the heart and reveal that truth lived at the bottom of a barrel; of mild ale that would drown the wits at the very moment of revelation. Ten paces distant down a narrow path, an alternative truth was offered at the Independent Chapel. Since most of the brethren had signed the pledge, The Bull's Head nodded to them in vain. Only a cold north wind sometimes disturbed the peace of Meetings, for then the smell of hops drifted through the chapel windows and no amount of Sankey and Moody could drive it out.

Since Langton children lacked their own school, they walked a mile to the next parish. Bottom-of-the-village children started off first, moving lamely up the main street. Others attached themselves to these first nuclei, till out of the morning air larger groups crystallised. Still smelling of bed and bacon fat, boys and girls sought a group to hide in. As they gathered their wits, sucked a last bacon rind and rubbed the 'gown' from their eyes,

4

groups became volatile, exploded, fragmented and condensed into lesser groups. Social difference had subtly emerged; like was with like, and remained so till absorbed by the magnet school.

When school ended, a bubble of children squeezed from the school doors into the roadway, hovered for a moment, then burst. Colourful groups spun erratically round, bound briefly by sheer pleasure. Then on the way home, these dissolved and regrouped till the social patterns were recreated by the time that home was reached.

When the weather was fine, poor children played in the street. When energy flagged they rushed briefly indoors, emerging always with food: a round of bread-and-jam, grasped two-handed, an apple, a stick of rhubarb or a carrot. Monotony pervaded all their games. Boys whipped tops, grew bored and whipped one another round bare legs, for garters were mostly absent. Games of marbles ended in fights when drains swallowed up the best 'stripeys'. Some boys played leapfrog, till the frogs jerked up and threw the leapers backwards. Only cricket sustained any length of interest, and that against all the odds, with a soft rubber ball, wickets chalked on a wall, and a barrel stave for a bat. A village boy, idiot in all but name, was always appointed chief fielder and ran till he foamed at the mouth. He was rewarded with a chance to bat at the end but was usually fooled out before he had really begun.

Girls skipped to meaningless jingles parroted from mothers who had not understood them either. Some played hopscotch and always a few would brighten the hour by parading in mother's shoes. Other girls of thirteen or so gathered in tight little groups, weaving a web of fancy about boys older than themselves who had gone into long trousers after leaving school. Like their elder sisters, these girls knew that the war had left a surplus of women. It was never too soon to practise their feminine wiles. Sometimes in twos and threes they walked the length of the village street. Brave ones would place a celandine or a dogrose in their hair ribbons, undo the top buttons of their blouses and practise a mincing walk quite alien to their normal shambling gait. They need not have worried. None of the poorer girls was ever 'left on the shelf' to my knowledge. Indeed they were taken down and dusted far too soon. The natural animal charm of their late 'teens they used to good advantage and the youths were highly vulnerable. If they had a job they were considered 'a fair cop'. These early marriages made it difficult to sort out the generations. Grandmothers were often in their thirties. If a girl had a child and the father escaped marriage or was unknown, the infant was 'run in' with grandma's children. When the girl eventually found a husband, he was usually willing to take over the earlier offspring. Most marriages were still in church and white weddings too at any cost. This gave some sort of social gloss even to the most heavily pregnant girl. In the marriage ceremony at least, the poor could imitate their betters, and sometimes even produce a prettier bride.

Our village could boast, though many could not, a waterborne sewerage system. However, most poorer folk were not connected and some even balked at the idea of 'doing your business' indoors; perhaps with good reason since their cottages were so small. With a rare mixture of thrift and practicality, they dug a trench across the garden and emptied the toilet bucket into it. Since the privy was also in the garden, this was no great task. The waste was covered with a spit or two of soil and the garden was fertilised in the process. I knew of two brothers living on their own at a lodge farm who had a variant of this technique. They placed the wooden privy (doorless, so they could shepherd as they sat) over a pre-dug trench and moved the privy along week by week.

We had two flush toilets, one indoors and one outside. The former was largely reserved for the women folk, while the men used the one in the garden. At night we had chamber pots under the bed and in the event of illness there was a commode. Our London cousins often came to stay on the farm in summertime. In after years they remembered above all things the garden toilet. The Virginia creeper which camouflaged the outside wall, frequently strayed inside through the vent space over the door. With the door ajar, one looked at the south-facing end of the house where a peach tree fruited every year. One also commanded a view of the garden with plum and pear trees. Beyond these still were the farmyard buildings, and as one sat enthroned, feet on a square wooden block, it was possible to follow the events of the working day; to hear the men calling to the animals; to hear the rearing calves in converse with their mothers, and the cockerel challenging his neighbours up the village. Occasionally, if one lingered at a busy time, a voice from amongst the farm buildings would shout, 'Ready when you are.' This was the signal to put down yesterday's paper or the old copy of *The Farmer and Stockbreeder*, and get on with the real business of the day. 'There is a time for everything under the sun,' says the poem. For us it was mainly a time for work.

Home Farm

HALFWAY up Langton main street dwelt the eleven Cramps: a team folks called us, though I was never quite sure where I played. 'Follow the muck off the wagon wheels and you'll finish up in their yard' was the advice to enquiring strangers and for afterthought, 'Watch out or you'll finish up milking a cow.' Truly milk, muck and work, were the hallmarks of our trade.

Our house stood end-on to the road. A blanked-off window high in the gable end turned a blind eye on the village scene. Tramline cart ruts between overgrown limetrees led past the frontage, trapping land we called garden between drive and house. Ragged quilts of flowers appeared in due season for Nature was always head gardener. Snowdrop, violet, and daffodil insisted on annual visits despite cats, dogs, children and transgressing calves. Perennial sweet peas, and roses old as the house propped up the garden fence. Where garden joined house was never clear. Foundations grew from a bed of fern; frogs dwelt in the air vents. Maidenhair fern crept up the walls while tongues of lichen, yellow as the sandstone, marked the way for the next advance. Snails like outriders left silver trails that reached for the bedroom windows. Where ragged lines of mortar showed man once played a part, sparrows clung briefly in the afternoon sun, preened in the golden dust and for pleasure assaulted the stone. High under the eaves, mosses that delight in dripping gutters had begun their downward march, stretching damp fingers towards their friends below. Here and there, windows had grown moist green eyebrows, and as evening shadowed their face, they took on a melancholy rheumy look as if sad that age had darkened their sight. Sensing the mood, bats tumbled out of their dark stone chambers, and shrieked down the shadow paths cast by a westering sun.

Inside the citadel, quite unnoticing, our family teased out its destiny. Walls two feet thick would outlast our time, so the wrinkles of age were irrelevant. Yet sometimes even when very young, I felt oppressed by the past. I knew that the very stones had a story; that others had striven as we now did; and I wondered to what end. Had other boys plucked snails from their damp parlours, placed them on a leaf and watched how they pushed out glutinous horns; or found bats dry as leather hanging like bits of old harness in deep crevices? And up in the churchyard, was there buried a man who had touched the toad that lived under our laurel bush; a toad like a piece of stone gone bad, a wrinkled piece of death?

When I wondered aloud about past or future no one at home seemed anxious to listen. 'Sufficient unto the day,' was the clamant message that pervaded daily life. Only grandfather, rich in wisdom and years, encouraged me still to wonder. And I trusted him for he had scaled to the top of life's mountain and welcomed his growing glimpse of eternity.

A century of muck from midden and byre had lifted the kitchen garden to the height of its old stone wall. There in the summer, fruitful, quite splendid, and slightly unreal, was our own hanging garden of Babylon. As one walked up the drive past the sagging wall, earth stood headhigh; one glimpsed bush arcades, a worm's eye view of forbidden places like the sight of old ladies' legs beneath a green cloth-covered table. Bushes of blackcurrant and gooseberry embraced, grew into one another and lifted arms to the sun. A climb up six steps to the garden itself revealed a solid green jungle. Gooseberries, large as walnuts, veined and translucent, hung with blackcurrants in rich cornucopias. What plunder was here for small boys! We crawled unseen along moist bush tunnels and surfaced where fruit grew thickest; then down again

9

like moles with none but an errant thrush for company, or a ravening wolf in the form of Nipper the terrier, glad to be on licking level with his best friends.

In a 'jungle clearing' vegetables grew: cabbages so big that one served a meal for eleven, so solid we split them with a chopper; lettuces big as footballs and runner beans lacing the trellis like organ pipes. These and much more delighted mother though she had quite a job defending her cabbages when father had a sick cow. And late in the season, as all boys know, bean seeds make fine ammunition for catapults.

Between the two gardens and serving the kitchen was once a small cobbled yard. But the stones had retreated under countless feet and the path to the kitchen was now silted over, rippled like damp sand at low tide. A water pump, handle forever aloft, stood in permanent anticipation, while milk churns queued at its side, waiting their turn to be cleaned.

On up the drive past house and garden, the pulsing life of the farm: cows, calves, horses, poultry engaged in morning gossip. A pony whinnies. It starts with a high pitched rippling note, shivers down the scale and finishes with a velvet purr, soft as its own nose which greets us over the stable door. If she playfully grabs your shoulder or swipes a clover-scented kiss down the side of your face, a carrot top will be ample reward.

A little further on rank smells intrude, then thunderous bawling. Both are greetings from a choir of calves that stand on a raised stage of muck. Daily additions of straw to their bedding have so raised the floor of their byre that with much neck stretching they can peer goggle-eyed over their enclosing fence. Show your head over the door and they will do a ballet for you round their pen, then suddenly freeze as if waiting your applause. This is their brief youth: their future the dairy or fattening pastures, or soon the butcher's knife if demand for veal is good.

A comforting and comfortable sound is the muffled

crunch from milch cows, chewing down skeins of hay from their racks and giving an occasional damp cough when like hungry children they gobble too fast. You'll be lucky to see their heads for they stand square-hipped, backs to the viewer down the length of their shed — a vista of udders and gently swishing tails, and over all the smell of cow. Yet here notwithstanding, is the source of much of our wealth. The cowsheds are our temples, the smell of milk and dung a daily incense. No Hindoo holds the cow in greater esteem than we do, and daylong we dance attention on them. We are often the beasts of burden, with yokes on our shoulders and balanced buckets of forage and water. When I was six or seven I held a fork (made specially by the blacksmith) as easily as a pencil. So rough and calloused did my hands become at week-ends that in Monday morning school I had the utmost difficulty in writing for the first hour or two.

Few domestic animals display more appetite than a cow in full milk. In winter ours were fed mainly indoors, so into the sheds we lugged water and hay, mangolds, cattle cake and straw bedding: out came milk and muck. For convenience, the latter was heaped on a concrete apron close by the cowsheds. Only when it grew to ava-lanche proportions, with rich brown liquor draining from shiny black glaciers, was it carted away to the main farm and spread. But always there was work that only a pair of hands could do, and my elder brothers had hands like shovels. It was said that when farm workers held their partners in dance, the right hand obscured the lady's back.

The monthly milk cheque was the family drip-feed that seemed to keep us alive. If it hadn't arrived by the seventh of the month we made the postman search his bag; and the family mood could not have been worse if the cows had gone on strike.

In return for their milk, the cows received the best of medical attention; far better than that so grudgingly given to their human masters. We had few medicines for family use: to be ill was an anti-social interruption of the farm routine. But for cows there was a veritable pharmacopoeia of medicaments, as well as syringes and other equipment usually kept in the kitchen. The cowshed cabinet could have doctored a zoo, and we all had great faith in its contents. Bottles were deeply ridged, specially for farmers' horny hands to grip, and each bore a graphic label. Not even the illiterate could mistake the head of a sneezing horse or a calf with its tail up, 'pumping out'. The picture that gripped my fancy most was a cloud of bluebottles over the back of a sheep indicating maggots and fly-blown flesh; much more apt I thought than the swarm of bees on the tins of treacle mother bought. Instructions on bottles were equally vivid. Favourites were 'apply freely to affected parts' or 'add contents to a pint of gruel and give as a drench'. The wise might have added, 'First catch your bullock.'

Half the village had faith in our cures for cuts, bruises and sprains. Udder salves, blue Vaseline, iodine and horse liniment doctored both man and beast. They leaked from the farm via our man. But mother insisted that, while slippage was within reason, it should not be stopped, considering how so many benefited. She said the same of molasses, fed to the cows. When watered down, we heard, it made fine treacle pudding.

With no disrespect to womankind, father would sometimes emphasise certain similarities between cows and women. Well-shaped udders like well-formed breasts were good selling points. Both cows and women responded to fuss and good food when pregnant. There was some similarity in the problems experienced before, during and after giving birth: Caesarean births, milk fever and sore teats were common to both. Both lost their early good figure after producing several offspring and tended to middle-age spread. However, not to offend his listener, father always added, 'But where should we all have been without the ladies?'

More than once I have crawled from my warm feather pit in the middle of the night to help with a difficult calving, to haul on pulleys or steady the calf as it 'dropped' onto heaps of straw. I have watched with amazement a calf's first sneeze and his magic response to the first massage of his mother's rasping tongue, all long before I was twelve. It was after such interrupted nights I was allowed to sleep late in the morning. Breakfast was kept specially warm, and that was honour indeed.

Cows in milk have a special sense of their own importance as every motorist on a country lane knows. Perhaps it derives from the good food, regular meals and kind treatment meted out to these creatures that put milk in our tea and butter on our bread. They seem to know they are earning a living for the owner and hence can claim certain concessions. Being ladies they insist on a certain decorum. Full udders certainly make running difficult, but they take advantage and try to make their own rules. How exasperating they often were on summer evenings! Home, dog-tired from the hayfield, I could 'Coop, coop, coop', like a dog baying at the moon, hoping they'd start to trail home to the sheds. Not a bit of it! Though their udders were tight as drums and teats were oozing milk, they would continue enjoying the dewy grass as if I didn't exist. It was useless to send Floss, the shepherd dog. They knew her bark was worse than her bite and ignored her. At best they hastened a step or two, then heads down again. Not till I got right amongst them, shouted and waved a stick would the homeward trek start at funeral pace. To add to the insult, milking over, they rushed back to the pasture at twice the pace, with Floss barking hard and recovering prestige by pretending she hastened the exit.

Signing a milk agreement with the wholesalers, brought annual family agonising. We were in their hands totally for disposal of milk and well they knew it. While not daring to refuse their offer, we still fought for an

extra halfpenny or farthing a gallon. Mr Micawber would
have appreciated our dilemma. Farthings multiplied up
significantly in a year. To offset low prices in time of glut,
our answer ironically was to produce more with special
attention to plentiful water supplies. In the drought of
1921, we were first to employ a water diviner and sink
wells. But we were never driven to the expedients adopted
by some desperate farmers. Milk was poured into large
conical churns for collection. Inside on a brass strip were
special marks, indicating gallons, halves and quarters. I
knew one farmer who regularly increased his tally of milk.
With a sledge hammer he bashed large shallow dents in
the churn to raise the level of the milk. Others with more
subtlety added water. Scarcely a month passed but one
or another was brought before the local court. Most of the
magistrates were local gentry who hunted over the farms
and knew that times were hard. They were usually
sympathetic, for as the farmers said, 'We all piddle in the
same pot.' More frequent than small fines were warnings
to see that the workmen 'drained the churns thoroughly
after washing'. A nod was as good as a wink.

Summertime was flytime on the farm, and well the
milkers knew it. Handmilking is normally relaxing unless
it goes on hour after hour. The three-legged stool allows
the milker to grip the bucket between his knees leaving
both hands free. His head pressed firmly into the cow's
flank, the teats are rhythmically squeezed and pulled and
the milk jerks out in pencil-thick streams, making a comfortable sound as it froths in the bucket; peace reigns.
Then, bang! The cow swings her tail at the flies on her
rump. Being summer, the muck on the end of her tail
has dried hard as bullets and smites the milker hard
round the face. If you're still on the stool with bucket
intact, you're lucky. The cure is to tie the tail to the back
leg and put up with a fidgeting cow.

Two farmyard sounds ring in my memory over all the
years. For pride, nothing exceeds the cockerel, seen and

heard at close quarters as he launches a challenge to every cock within half a mile. Neck outstretched and comb aflame he shrills, 'This is my harem; I'm boss here.' Or as we used to mock him, 'Ca-come-and-I'll-do-for-you.' But for pathos, there is the bleat of a lost lamb at sunset: sad as an evening wind blowing through marsh reeds, and quite without hope. Perhaps the sound that Mother liked best was that of a cackling hen announcing another egg. Since Father provided the hens and the corn, eggs were net gain to Mother. Not only were there enough for the house, but eggs were Mother's currency, as cowrie shells are to some remote islanders. Whenever there were minor debts to settle with local people they were given the choice of cash or eggs. The latter was always the best buy and all the village knew it. So eggs paid for the knitting of socks and scarves, the making and altering of dresses, sweeping the chimneys, and beating of carpets. Eggs were frequent gifts to the old and sick; they were perched in church windows at harvest festival and provided prizes for local whist drives. They rewarded children who brought posies in springtime and were given to many a 'traveller' who called on business, and had the misfortune, as Mother said, to live in a town.

Clearly Mother had no time for foxes; they were robbers ready to break into her bank, a threat to her way of life. She was certain they watched her drive to market, for twice they had plundered on Tuesdays. As a counter-measure she kept her pullets in four different huts: the fox was usually content with one. He sometimes came in broad daylight, parading his ruddy coat among Mother's Rhode Island Reds, and as I believe, loving the excitement. The silly hens seemed oblivious to danger till a neck or two were broken, when they scattered far and wide. The fox can kill with a single chop on the neck. Once in a roost he would kill the lot though he only took one or two away. Next morning, only the odd feather blowing across neighbouring fields gave a general idea of the lair; but that could be miles away. The dead birds were good to eat, and the villagers had cheap chicken for days.

However, all was not lost. Our farm straddled the Fernie Hunt country; no Hunt exists without the goodwill of the farmer and that often meant his wife. So Mother received compensation, bought more pullets, reopened 'the poultry bank', issued new egg currency and traded happily till the vaults were raided again. Father was the fox's best friend. When their bark 'Hoo-hooed' through the frosty air on a Winter's night, and Mother paused from her sewing, Father would say, 'Listen to that old owl,' and poke the fire noisily. But on such nights I noticed he always left the dog unchained! His reaction was sound business instinct. The hunting fraternity bought our hay and clover: they paid promptly and never queried the price. It paid us to graze their hunters in summertime; and they gave us horses they did not need. So we all learned to 'hack', and broke in strong hunters to work in shafts. Every animal, cat, dog, or horse, had to earn its keep.

Village Folk

U P TO THE AGE OF TEN, my heroes varied from week to week. There was the railway ganger whom I met when taking milk to the station. He would balance a sixpence on a pin stuck in a railway sleeper, and dislodge the coin with his great hammer without ever disturbing the pin. There was the local farmer who fought off a bull with a hayfork in the middle of a field, and saved his own son; and the hedgecutter who walked all the way home gripping his own wrist to save himself from bleeding to death. I thought they all deserved the Victoria Cross.

But with the growing sensitivity of adolescence came a deepening interest in the persons and personalities of my village. Sometimes, when lying in bed at night, I would go all round the village, house by house, and imagine what each family was doing and saying. By day, I listened to any who would talk, especially about their work or their own childhood.

In the 1920s our village was still fairly isolated. Spasmodically there were attempts to run buses to local towns, but few of the workers had money to spend on the fare or on entertainment in the town. So demand was slight and no sooner was a service begun than it ceased. Few folk seemed able to afford even a bicycle, so for the most part they walked when going to work, to evening entertainment in local villages, or to the railway station two miles away. They took advantage too, of numerous footpaths which crisscrossed the countryside. It was even possible to move from one end of the village to the other without passing down the main street, by using field paths that ran at the back of the houses. Some said that these paths had originated with people who attended the Independent Chapel at the top of the village but found it wise not to parade their intentions before the Anglicans.

Comparative isolation breeds individuality; in the absence of mass media our village folk were still not stamped with a standard culture. Few labourers could read sufficiently well to make it worth while to take a daily paper, even if they could have afforded one. But most of them still bought *Olde Moore's Almanac*, which was hawked around by gypsies. Its mixture of fact, folklore and prophecy provided talking points for weeks. But most people were truly themselves. Had they not been so, village life would have lacked the variety and richness which made life tolerable for so many.

One of the unforgettable characters of my childhood was Mr Busby. His billheads boasted, and with good reason, that he was 'Frank Zacharias Busby, Wheelwright, Joiner, Painter, Decorator and Undertaker'. Locals called him Zach. Befitting a man with such Biblical overtones, he was a pillar of the church. It also seemed appropriate that my father and he should always address one another as 'neighbour', a form of address used nowhere else in the village. Zach's house and workshops lay at the bottom of the village about a hundred yards from our farmhouse. But to visit them was to enter another world. Entrance to his property put me in mind of entering a castle. His house was linked to a neighbouring one by an arch over which was a bedroom. The arch was big enough to admit the largest farm wagons and led to a spacious yard. One side was flanked by a wing of the house and extending from it was a long range of buildings.

First came the wheelwright's shed round which was ranged every item that goes to make a wheel: seasoned wood, spokes, fellies, hubs, hub caps and iron rims. There was usually a wheel on the floor, assembled in all particulars except for the rim. The securing of this was for me one of the wonders of the world. Outside the workshop at ground level was a flat round iron plate large enough to accommodate a cartwheel and with a hole in the centre to receive the hub. It was pivoted over a shallow waterbath. The wooden wheel was laid on the iron plate. Meanwhile, in a high and narrow oven was the iron rim, being evenly heated and expanding as it did so. Then came the exciting part. The rim was pulled from the oven with iron tongs and skilfully dropped over the wooden wheel with just enough clearance all round. Then at the pull of a lever, plate, wheel and rim were submerged in the bath. For a moment the water bubbled and steamed, the iron rim shrank and every joint in the wooden wheel was inexorably squeezed into place, with never a piece of wood splitting.

Next to the wheelwright's shop lay the paint shop. No Aladdin's cave could have boasted a finer entrance. The brickwork on either side of the doorway was no longer discernible, but glistened with paint of every hue. This was the place where paint brushes were cleaned off prior to rinsing in turpentine or immersion in water. For half a century, reds, blues, greens, whites, yellows and a myriad other colours had been wiped onto the brickwork. Colour overlay colour at random. Here and there the very depth of the paint gave an effect that was jewel-like and solid. Ruby, emerald and sapphire shone from a bed of scrambled rainbows. I wondered if tired apprentices had appreciated the effect as I did. The paint shop, some twenty feet square, was lined with shelves which held tins of every shape and size. On some, the label had yellowed and curled, so one could only guess the contents from paint traces on the rim. Some tins were so rusted one wondered if even Zach knew the contents. Clearly labelled were varnishes, woodstains, dyes for colouring whitewash, glue, priming paint, and glosspaint in profusion. Zach was equally at home varnishing a cart or a coffin, painting a farm gate or a house interior, colourwashing a cottage or a church interior. To this day, I can never smell glue without recalling a vision of Zach, blue eyed, fair haired and short of stature, watching his three-legged iron pot as the water in it gurgled round the inner pot, which held the glue.

'What does Mother need today?' He smiled knowingly. Like everyone else in the village he knew that on matters domestic Mother's word was law and she would brook no delay. 'Mother's spring cleaning,' I blurted out. No other words of mine were needed to convey to him the urgency of my situation. He lowered the flame under the glue and gave me his whole attention. 'It's the dining room,' I said. 'Mother thinks it's too dark. She says you will know what will brighten it up and go with the furniture and the carpet.' Know, indeed. How could he fail to? Every house of consequence in the village and many of the humbler cottages too, bore his imprint, and he knew every room in the houses he visited. He knew the colour, shape and approximate dimensions; where he had fixed a cupboard or a shelf, reglazed a window, renewed a floor, papered or colour-washed a wall.

'Ah,' said Zach knowingly, 'I've got just the colour — old gold.' He promptly mixed a little white-based colour wash and added the old gold stainer, stirred it and poured a little into a tin. 'Let your Mother try this sample,' he smiled. 'I'm sure she'll approve.' Mother did, so back I ran for the full mix. Years later he confided to me one of the secrets of his trade as decorator. 'When folks don't know what colour to have, old gold is the answer. It's not too dark, not too light, and covers well and goes with most things; like a gold watch or a gold ring, never out of place.' How right he was. It is safe to assert that most houses in our village had at least one old gold room, and it was also a favourite for halls and passageways. To this day, my favourite room, a south-facing lounge, has a plain paper washed over with a colour that must please Zach.

No modern undertaker could give the kind of personal service rendered by Zach, for he was so much part of the community he served. When folks died, he attended to the special needs of the family just as effectively as when he decorated their cottage or repaired their farm cart. He knew instinctively that in a village one's life is open to closer scrutiny than in the confessional box. He was not a specialist like modern undertakers; he was first and foremost a village dweller. That being so, every job would be special, for his customers were people with needs and feelings like his own. His humanity was reflected in his carpenter's shop. Here and there, pinned on beams and window frames, were short poems, aphorisms and jingles, which over the years had taken his fancy. Perhaps to encourage his apprentice there was, 'He who makes no mistakes makes nothing.' In more serious vein was,

> Here is the man who planted the tree
> To grow in beauty for all to see.
> Here is the man who daily prayed
> Yet put that beauty to the blade.
> Here is the man who shaped the wood
> Made planks where earlier beauty stood.
> What is Man who from earth's womb
> Took beauty for his wooden tomb?

Stacked horizontally on racks along one side of the workshop were cut planks in various stages of seasoning for coffin making. Potential customers could choose from oak, elm or pine, according to their taste and their pocket. Likewise there was a choice of ornamental fitments in brass. But why such finery should be attached to a coffin and buried six feet deep within hours, I never could fathom. I had a sneaking sympathy for Thomas Hardy's poor country fellow who could see no reason why the dead should deprive the living of pleasure when the pennies placed on the eyes of the dead could buy good ale for the living. Yet I suppose Zach was right when he said that the body should be decently disposed of, for it once housed a soul.

For most of my childhood, coffins were carried shoulder high from hearse to church, often by farm workers who regarded the job as something of a perk, since they were by custom paid for it but suffered no deduction from wages. Later, a four-wheeled bier came into use, though it seemed to me to lack the dignity of a man carried by his fellows, besides being an unnecessary piece of technology which deprived men of a job.

At the bottom of the village, not far from the manor, were two cottages, each housing an elderly married couple. The two men worked as servants at the manor; no woman ever stayed more than a week. Between them, they did all the cooking, cleaning, and odd-jobbing. They were easily identifiable because they always moved at something between a walk and a run. This satisfied their mistress, as it gave every appearance that they were willing to break into a full-blooded sprint if she gave the word. One of these poor fellows was called 'Chinnerman Charles'; his chin was in continual motion as if in silent speech. Those who purported to know him best said he maintained under his breath a non-stop 'Yes madam, yes madam, immediately madam', and even spoke it in his sleep. Such was the price paid by some for keeping a roof over their heads, for most farm workers lived in 'tied' cottages.

Next to Zach Busby's workshops were a pair of attractive farm workers' cottages. Within living memory, they had once formed the Chequers Inn. The smell of ale still haunted every room, and would forever, it was said. One tenant, George Bailey, assured me it was a daily misery to come home from the fields, and to be greeted by the wonderful aroma of hops but without so much as a pint of the real thing to moisten his lips. He still had the old inn sign hanging on his bedroom wall.

Beyond old Bailey's house, a field ran up to the village street. In the absence of a barbed-wire back fence, inquisitive bullocks would line up and press so far into the roadside hedge that their heads protruded over the pathway. Some would stand while their heads were scratched but this became a less popular pastime when a number of

Tur Langton across the fields of ridge and furrow, dominated by its redbrick, 1860s church

The eleven Cramps. The Author is on the left in front

Brother Bob in the orchard, 1920. The hero of the family, he survived the trench warfare of World War I and is still farming today

Sister Muriel – 'a stunner for looks and knew it' – on a Francis Barnet

Father 'shoulder high to a bullock'

children contracted ringworm and one poor boy lost a patch of his hair.

Opposite the field was the house of Police Sergeant Barker. The notice boards outside his house seemed chiefly to display warnings about birds whose eggs it was prohibited to take. I never thought of them having any relevance to myself, perhaps because the Sergeant's son was as keen a collector as any of us. There was other small-print stuff too, but nobody ever read it. Even the notice about sheep dipping was redundant, for the Sergeant visited every farm house personally and supped a bottle of ale at each. He was zealous in watching for poachers at night. In this, however, he had a vested interest, for he had permission from several farmers to go rabbiting on their farms. He did his rounds on a three-speed bicycle, riding sedately, and, it seemed, always in top gear to maintain his pompous image. Old village photographs which include him show his right arm well twisted forward, that all should know of his rank. I could never stomach him after a story his daughter told me. Returning home one summer afternoon, he asked her if she had been eating the raspberries. Disbelieving her denial, he made her open her mouth while he examined her teeth. He found no seeds. What he did not know was that the trace of red on Mary's lips which gave rise to his suspicions was the remains of lipstick, hurriedly removed, for when her father went on duty, she often went courting with a village boy in a nearby disused and overgrown sandpit.

About halfway up the village, and next door to our own house, stood the village post office, an ancient stone building with decayed and tattered thatch which sat like a wet hat on an impoverished owner. Only close scrutiny revealed that the house was in any way special. The red letter box bearing the monogram of Queen Victoria was camouflaged by its red sandstone setting. In the only ground-level window facing the road was a framed notice telling of office opening hours. This contended for space with round glass jars containing humbugs, striped mints, barley sugars, toffees, bulls' eyes and strips of Spanish juice which we called wiggy-waggy; for Mrs Ward combined sweetshop with post office. When customers pushed open the door, a rusty bell summoned her from the back regions, but her arrival was always delayed, for, with the help of a handicapped son, she also ran a smallholding and kept cows. One had to allow time for her to come from henhouse, midden, cowshed or kitchen, and hopefully, time to wash her hands. My visits were chiefly for sweets: ha'porths and penn'orths. Despite the glass-stoppered bottles, the sweets seemed always to become congealed; so Mrs Ward had usually to plunge a calloused hand into the bottle to wrest a lump from the main mass. This in turn had sometimes to be tapped with a small hammer to produce the fractional amounts we children ordered. Indeed the cracking-up process would have scattered the profits over the shop floor, had not the lady resorted to the device of lapping the sweets or toffees in her apron while she smote them. If it was the indoor apron, I didn't mind, but when her approach down the corridor was preceded by the damp slapping of her outdoor hessian apron, I changed my mind to something that needed no use of the brass hammer. I lived with farm smells, but cowhair or worse on a well-earned toffee lump was heresy. Our purchases were sometimes in farthings, which were still in regular use by the grocer, the milkman and the baker, and often figured in church collections.

The post office telephone was mainly used by the better-off people. Mrs Ward would wind the black handle and obtain the exchange before leaving the client to continue business. But there was little privacy, for the door of the booth was wedged half open by an uneven brick floor. Thus, through phone and telegrams, Mrs Ward became privy to many a secret. Via the postman she also had news from the world beyond our village. For these reasons she was regarded with more respect than her humble setting might suggest.

A favourite character of mine was Mrs Bagshaw, who lived at the bottom of the village in a pleasant terraced cottage owned by the manor house. I never heard that she had had any professional training, but she had acted as midwife to most families in the village, while the local doctors found her useful, competent and literate. During the years that I knew her, she always appeared the same — neither old nor young, but on an unshakable plateau between these two states. Her dress was the same whatever the hour of the day or the season of the year: black skirt, black blouse, shoes and stockings, relieved only by a white cameo brooch and a white shawl. Outside the house she wore a black cape and carried a black umbrella. Besides attending confinements she would act as nurse for the richer families, doing a night shift when there was serious illness. When poor people were ill and trying to conceal it, she would send a private message via the postman to the doctor, who trusted her judgement. Our village was fortunate in having an eighteenth-century charitable foundation. This helped to defray the cost of medical and hospital treatment for the needy, but the likes of Mrs Bagshaw were the first and often free providers for the sick. Most times when I met her out of doors, cape pulled around her, she would say, 'It's piercin', Harold.' To this I sometimes made the provocative reply, 'Piercin' hot or piercin' cold, Mrs Bagshaw?' Her reply was always, 'Piercin' cold lad: heat don't pierce.' She was found dead in her rocking chair, shawl still round her shoulders.

'Robbo' lived by himself in a cottage with a single-brick wall and a mud floor. His real name was Robinson but our nickname was appropriate, since he spent his time trapping singing birds on limed twigs, and selling them in the city. No one knew his precise origin but it was said he had once been tried for murder and acquitted. He also ate birds which he shot with an airgun. Over the years he developed the habit of sucking the lead pellets he fired. He even offered them to friends as one might offer snuff. One day, a friend who lived opposite Robbo was alarmed when first one window pane cracked, and then another. Going outside to investigate, he noticed the muzzle of Robbo's gun sticking through his cottage window. He found the old man on his bed under the window, in his one and only downstairs room. He had used his last ounce of strength to summon help, but too late. A post-mortem revealed that he had died of acute lead poisoning and under-nourishment. He was one of very few in our village who must have lived at near starvation level, despite shooting birds and rabbits and gathering the fruits of the countryside and selling his birds. But it is doubtful if he ever went cold. His forays into the fields were disguised as 'going sticking' and indeed he did collect wood every day, so when winter came he had a vast pile of kindling in his back garden. Like many another poor person, he damped his fire down with coal slack and kept it going through the night.

A boisterous friendly man, who made a big impression on my early years, was Bill Rogers, the village blacksmith. If my days did not start with the rattle of milk churns, the crowing of cocks or the barking of dogs, they began with the penetrating and melodious ring of Bill's anvil. I knew, as did everyone else, exactly what he was doing. Not a man, woman or child who had not watched him shoeing farm-horses or hunters; for me the fascination never waned.

Bill's house lay a little higher up the village than our own. In high summer a casual observer might not be aware of a house at all, but rather of a green and tousled mass, with here and there a fleck of colour. The effect was produced by Virginia creeper, with which climbing roses fought a losing battle as the summer drew on. The windows were small dark holes in the foliage, deep-set eyes. From over the doorway, a score of Virginia creeper tails hung down, challenging the visitor to part the leafy curtain and penetrate the cavernous porch behind. Once in this cool and leafy cave, concealment was complete. Whenever it was my good fortune to take a note to the smith about an intended shoeing, I went to this housedoor. I knew there would be no answer to my knocking, for his wife was as deaf as a post. But I could linger in the 'cave' and listen to the world outside, or finger the huge knocker, shaped like a horse's head. In the end, I had to face reality and go to the smithy.

This was built onto the end of the house and comprised two parts, the forge and the shoeing shop; the latter was cobbled, with doors open to the road day and night. Bill said horses stood best when there was something to claim their attention, and Bill was rarely without his admirers. He would start by removing the old shoe. Next the foot was pared with a wicked-looking curved knife to remove surplus dead hoof and grit. Then came the shoeing proper. Since every horse was a regular client, he knew the foot size and shape and had shoes already made to measure for fitting. First a cold matching of shoe to foot. Then into the forge went the shoe for heating, hammering and final bedding. The hot shoe was pressed to the foot, burning a firm seating and emitting pungent grey fumes as it sizzled into place. Then came the nailing, upwards through shoe and hoof, and out at the side of the hoof. Protruding nail ends were cut off and smoothed with a file. Finally the hoof was anointed with oil. At the nailing stage I was always fearful lest the nail drove into living tissue. Bill would have been shocked at such a thought.

Like the smith immortalised in poetry, Bill was a mighty man. A sense of enormous strength was conveyed, not so much by his muscles as by his veins. They stood out from his white and sweat-cleansed skin like blue cords. His arms and hands were laced with them, his neck seemed to be supported by them, and they stood out on his brow like a living blue wreath. As shoeing progressed, these veins distended, till I thought his temples would burst.

Bill's real *tour de force* was when he shod pedigree stallions that were based in our village for stud. These 'entire' horses were giants, weighing a ton. When shoeing them, Bill had not only to bend double, but also 'make a knee' on which the horse's foot rested when it was lifted and bent backwards. Rarely did he use a wooden support block. From his bent position, Bill picked up nails with his left hand and hammered them in with his right. Now there's scarcely a horse living that will not, when placed in the shoeing position, try gradually to distribute some weight onto the foot being shod, that is, onto the smith. Bill worked in a lather of sweat and a halo of words, many of his own coinage, and directed at the horse to make him take his own weight. None was a swear word that I knew, and I knew most. But Bill never really lost his temper, and thereby hangs a tale.

As a young apprentice elsewhere, he had been extremely wild, often roaring drunk and violent with it, till the day he was involved in a brawl and one man died. This so frightened him that he signed the pledge. From that day forward, he neither drank nor swore – except in the way I have described. His great strength he expended in shoeing and making shoes; he beat the hot iron with a terrifying vigour; sparks flew to the very door of the forge. The sweat from his brow dripped and sizzled on the glowing metal as he kept up his tattoo. Bill was toughening the iron which was to spend its life with a ton of horse-flesh above it, and a rough metalled road below. But I thought he was also toughening his soul and literally knocking hell out of himself. And when he finally straightened his back from the anvil and wiped his face with a rough hessian towel, he looked spiritually as well as physically cleansed, and his twinkling pale blue eyes said so.

There was one occasion when Bill did lose his temper and it was then that he performed the greatest feat of strength ever known in our village. According to an eye witness, he hooked his arms round his massive anvil and jerked it through the smithy window with a roar that could be heard the length of the main street. It fell on the cobbles outside and, to Bill's horror, vanished. He must have thought he had an unsolicited return of the D Ts, for he fled down the passage at the side of his smithy and into his house. A few minutes later, he returned, pale and trembling, but confident of his senses. The anvil had descended on the top of an ancient well, punched a hole through the cobbles, and fallen twenty feet to the bottom. Bill's roar had drawn an immediate audience from the Crown Inn opposite. Apparently one half-drunk fellow came across and was only saved from following the anvil by a sober friend. Another man, through necessity or desire, made water into the well, swearing the while that he could gauge the depth by the echo from the bottom. It seems the arrival of the smith's daughter soon put an end to the scene though, living opposite the pub, she did not lack enlightenment. She knew why neither weed nor flower would grow round the pub walls, why Dolly Thornton with but a small old age pension to live on could get gin galore from the publican, and why the post-man called at the house of Mrs Taylor, though she was nearly illiterate.

It took two days to recover the anvil: one to secure a hawser over the heel and toe, and another to erect a winch over the wellhead. No one ever found out what had upset Bill. Some said he was mad because his wife had given him a bad egg for breakfast. Years later, his daughter said that the sight of beer drinkers through the pub window opposite brought such a great temptation on him that hurling the anvil through the window was his way of proving that he could subdue the flesh and shame the Devil.

How can a sober masterbaker and smallholder work hard seven days a week all his life and die virtually penniless? Well, our village baker did. He had a heart of gold and supplied the daily bread of half-a-dozen villages from his small bakery. I got to know him well on two counts. First, he was my godfather, which happened as follows. I was born in April on St George's Day, in the middle of the lambing season. It seems Father was far too busy to take time off for a christening, so my baptism was overlooked for sixteen years. It suddenly occurred to Mother one day that without baptism I could not be confirmed and without confirmation I would never get the support for University from the parson, who was M A, Oxon., and the lord of the manor who was a J P. So the autumn Sunday, following this maternal reasoning, was designated for my baptism. Father was prevailed on to accompany me to the service 'For those of Riper Years'. The name of the service, I felt, was a compliment, especially as I was able to slip in a name extra to the ones in which I had been registered at birth. That's how the 'Saint' came to precede the George.

On the way into church we chanced on Mr Freestone the baker, who was pressed into the service to be my godfather. Who else by chance I might have had, I would not care to speculate. I made my closer acquaintance with him every Saturday morning when I visited the bakery to collect seven pounds of dough which mother made into cakes. I usually had a chance to talk and sometimes to help. The bakehouse contained a brick oven which would take about fifty loaves at a time. It was fired from below with wood and coal. I learned something about most processes in the baking. My favourite job was to slice the dough in pieces for 'quartern' loaves and weigh it. I never acquired the baker's skill in kneading two loaves at a time. I did learn the art of hurling a burning spill into the dark tunnel of an oven, to place the tins correctly, and extract them all when baked, with a long-handled wooden shovel.

And the worst job? Well, the dough was allowed to rise in long wooden troughs lining the wall of the bakehouse. Despite their hinged lids, the troughs were often invaded by cockroaches, which had to be removed by hand. We hurled them into the oven fire, where they exploded with a lively pop. Even so, it was not unusual to find one insect or another entombed in a loaf. Since its origin was known, no customers seemed to worry particularly.

All the baker's customers had a bread book in which he entered the number of loaves delivered and the price — in pencil. He kept no master copy for himself. It was an open secret that the less scrupulous customers sometimes altered the book, ironically by using bread as an eraser. Yet every Christmas morning, every one who wished could take their extra-large pieces of meat or poultry to the bakehouse, where they were cooked to perfection. When Mr Freestone died he was in debt to the millers and, after the sale of his house and holding, there was next to nothing left. He laid up no treasure on earth, and of all the men I knew, most deserved the bread of life eternal.

Our postman came twice daily from Kibworth, by bicycle, making his deliveries as he proceeded up the village. Here and there he had cups of tea and sometimes delivered or collected shoes, for he was a cobbler in his spare time. His extended or frequent calls at some houses were often the subject of gossip. The more charitable said he was fond of tea, and, indeed, he regarded his job as both work and pleasure. He helped many a person to write a business letter, or complete an official form, and he was a mine of information about the shops in town where the best buys were to be had. At Christmas time he was too laden to ride his bicycle. It dripped with parcels and he took hours to go the length of the village. Through intimate personal knowledge of the recipients he knew the origin of every package and often its contents. He commiserated when an expected gift failed to turn up, and rejoiced when he could deliver something specially large or interesting. Round about the Christmas festival, many households regaled him with wine, to the chagrin of the folk at the top of the village who watched his snail's progress from their doorways. Their hearts sank with his diminishing load, and complaints were shouted from door to door. 'Ain't had our gal's parcel yet. She's in good service and posts it reg'lar. Should 'a come yesterday. Postman's probably so boozed by now he's gi'n it to that new lot at the bottom as never had a parcel in their life.' Another would add, 'I ain't forgot what happened four years ago when he took my parcel to the other Bodley crowd. 'Twere clearly stamped "London" and they knew as how they hadn't friends there. Doubtful if they got friends anywhere, but they tore it open and mauled everything afore they brought it up to me. And how do I know what were missing?'

There was often a moment of panic at the top of the village when the postman mounted his bike and rode off down the village. But it was only to collect a second bag of parcels left at the first house to ease delivery problems. So all was well in the end, and the elderberry wine 'up Shang-end' did the postman just as much good as the sloe gin and parsnip wine at 'Manor-end', for when he turned for home about mid-day, though minus his parcels, he was seen to be still wheeling his bicycle.

The postman was a regular caller at our house, being announced by the dog about eight o'clock. Apart from the usual flow of bills and circulars, and official forms to do with the farm, there were lots of personal letters. Mother was a prolific letter-writer, and at the centre of a wide correspondence network embracing both sides of the family.

The butcher visited our village during the week, but too early to bring any Sunday roast. In any case, mother scorned the 'gossip shop' which accompanied the butcher's high trap up the village. The meat he kept under the seat until he reached the village. Then he dropped the backboard and spread some of it out. The working-class women gathered round to make their choice. Some moved with the cart well up the village before deciding on a joint, partly to gossip, partly to see what others bought, but partly because some said the butcher tried to get rid of his rough stuff first, and they weren't going to have 'cow meat and scrag-end'.

When the butcher arrived at the bottom of our village, he hollered loudly to announce his presence. The '-cher' echoed in every house, the 'butch-' he said to himself. He was a vast man with a reddish-purple face. It was rumoured he drank bullocks' blood. It is certain he drank beer. His shout roused not only his customers to come to the door money in hand, but the publicans at the Bull's Head and the Crown. He took three pints at each, but to avoid delay they were lined up ready on the bar when he entered. It is not surprising that his exit from the village was a fine spectacle. His high-stepping horse struck showers of sparks from the metalled road, as he headed for the next village. With his whip held high, the butcher roared encouragement to the horse, no doubt to shorten the time to the next pints of ale. If speed of delivery had any effect, the meat was certainly fresh.

Occasionally tinkers and hawkers came through the village collecting rags, bones and scrap iron, in return for balloons, celluloid 'windmills' and other 'trumpery', as Mother called these knick-knacks. Whether induced not to call on us by the presence of the dog, or our reputation for thrift, I knew not. But the only balloon I had was made from a pig's bladder, and the only windmill I knew ground real corn. How could I forget, when I had to wait for hours with Father in the lee of the old post mill at Kibworth until the flour was ground?

A Grassy World

IN ALL the parish records, tax returns and county gazetteers, Hector C. Cramp, my father, was classified as a grazier. That truly describes him, for in his heaven there were no ploughed fields. Like the Psalmist he found comfort in the prospect of verdant pastures and quietly flowing waters, for in that haven cattle, cows and sheep could multiply and grow fat. The main part of our farm lay near the hamlet of Shangton, in the heart of Leicestershire. The farmhouse in Tur Langton was a mile away. It is gently rolling country with a stream in every valley, draining the dark clay soil. Here man and Nature seem embattled no longer but working to one harmonious plan. Ridge and furrow in endless green waves ripple across every field, pass beneath the hedges and continue on their way. Once they were 'furlongs' under the plough, in an open unfenced landscape, climbing the hills, descending to the valleys and finishing in 'headlands' where the plough turned. Now they are smooth green ribbings, stitched over with hawthorn hedges as a result of the Enclosure Act of 1800. Farms have become private empires of fenced fields, wearing a smug and comfortable look, and our farm was no exception. We were proud to display to visiting relatives an Ordnance Survey map which showed our every field and spinney and the two streams which intersected the farm. We owned a bit of England and we liked the idea, for as Father said, 'God doesn't make land any more.'

Yet Leicestershire's coat of rich herbage, and hawthorn hedges freely decked with ash and oak, deceives the eye. For underneath lies a harsh unyielding clay, the fruits of which must be dearly bought. A walk across our meadows soon proves that farmers see with their feet as well as their

34

eyes. In summer the clay bakes hard and to walk the fields is an ankle-breaking affair. One moment the foot rides a grassy pinnacle, the next it slides into cavernous footprints made by cattle the previous winter. These holes are beloved of nesting partridge and skylark, and squatting hares and rabbits, but they menace the mowing machine and can easily break a sheep's leg.

Most village houses were built of brick, baked from local clay, and many a floor was no more than beaten clay. A few mud-walled houses still survived. With deep thatch and tiny windows, they were scarcely distinguishable from cow byres. As old folk died off, sparrows demolished the thatch, walls fell in and only a grassy mound survived. 'Earth to earth . . . dust to dust' was as true of the dwelling place as the dwellers therein. Earth mounds, whether in churchyard or outside, are still after 2000 years some of man's most touching memorials.

Leicestershire archives record the Cramp family as yeoman farmers from the sixteenth century onwards mainly farming on the eastern edge of Charnwood Forest. Around 1800 an inventory appended to the will of Jonathan Cramp of Glenfield includes three wagons and nine horses on a substantial mixed holding. But the later nineteenth century brought less happy times. My grandfather told how liver fluke in sheep diminished the family fortunes and his father was reduced to acting as an assistant farm bailiff for the Burnaby family of Baggrave Hall. Hence Grandfather was forced to seek an apprenticeship in ecclesiastical wood carving. But with capital accumulated he soon resumed the family tradition with a small dairy farm at Kibworth Beauchamp. A few years on and he was able to help my father purchase the Tur Langton homestead and farm.

That my father was cast in the true family mould no one would be inclined to dispute, for to look at him dressed for work (and he was rarely dressed for anything else) was to look at history. One was not aware of any particular item of his clothing nor was there much change, whatever the season of the year. He exuded a timeless quality, as if he had always been around, and always would be. In barn, byre or field, he merged into his background. He was not so much a countryman as part of the country. For me, wind and weather were constraints; for Father they seemed a necessary and normal part of his working scene. When he worked outside in rain-sodden fields, he was the rain and the earth, seeming to take the essence of them into his person. Standing in a field with a flock of sheep around him, he became the archetypal shepherd. When he spoke to cows in their stalls, they stopped cudding and listened.

He belonged to a dying breed of farmer, for whom the whole of Nature was a listening post. He farmed by sense, rather than reason or science. He believed that you ignored the voice of Nature at your peril. He saw land as the ultimate resource, God-created and given to man in trust. So his pride in his farm would never allow him to regard it simply as a means to personal enrichment. Farming was a way of life rather than an exploitation of resources. His attitude to new farming techniques was ambivalent. Though he used up-to-date machinery, he regretted the need to do so, for the more sophisticated the tool, the greater the barrier between man and the earth. To the end of his days he loved to feel the swing of the scythe, to watch nettles, grass or thistles fall before its blade, and to smell the sap and the pollen released by his labour.

Father was stockily built and never seemed to tire. Between meals he never rested, never leaned on a gate, perched his backside on a sack of corn, reclined on a heap of hay or in any wise ceased to labour. Work was refreshment enough. His nearest approach to entertainment was attending the Christmas concert of local talent, and that, I suspect, because it was held in an old granary. When forced to stand still, his arms hung out slightly forward, with fingers forever outspread as if to grapple with an invisible ox. His feet stood apart, as if glued to the ground before he could bring them together. When he ran, which was rarely, it was with short stabbing steps, pumping his feet into the ground as if anxious not to lose contact. He never perspired, grunted or hoo-haa'd at his work as we boys so often did. It was as if the job just gave itself up when Father performed it. Watching him at work at the end of a day, when I could often have cried with fatigue, I used to wonder not when will he stop, but can he stop? No man could so tease out one job into another, as if the work links must never be broken even by sleep. And he went to bed threatening tomorrow with twice as much work as today. Friends remember the greasy cloth cap that he wore, waterproofed with oil from the flanks of a hundred cows, and worn with the pride of a knight's escutcheon. But more, they remember the laughing blue eyes which said that he nursed a secret. And he did — the joy of being exactly what he was.

We boys often found the task of matching his standards disheartening. There was rarely spoken criticism of our efforts; there was little praise either. Father simply assumed we would perform the tasks required of us, and the results would speak for themselves. If we said we had milked a cow and Father then 'stripped' another pint from it, what words were needed? If hungry pigs, even though ringed through the nose, rooted the door off their sty to get at apples in the orchard, someone who sat round the kitchen table was to blame for not feeding them. Our life seemed subordinate to that of the animal kingdom. We were ruled by cows, bullocks, horses, sheep, pigs and hens. Our meals were timed to suit theirs; we dressed to serve their needs; they were the main subject of our conversation. Day-long they bullied us with their bellowing, bawling, bleating, grunting and cackling, for the moment we neglected them they reported the fact to Father.

However, Father was equable and rarely raised his voice even in anger. Indeed any direct physical chastisement of us when young was left to Mother, who kept a little switch in the kitchen. Her edict ran within the house, its immediate environs and the gardens. So to escape her wrath we had only to flee across the border into Father's province, the farmyard, and we were safe. When we returned with Father at mealtime, and he mentioned the work we had done, our transgressions were quite forgotten.

Yeoman farmers down the ages have managed their farms with mainly family labour. We did likewise and rarely employed more than one outside labourer, excepting a few casuals at hay harvest. Nor did Father need more, with nine lusty children: seven boys and two girls. Though Mother certainly had no desire for so large a family, along we came at two-year intervals, but not one of us regretted by Father. Perhaps his frugal yeoman's sense made him determined to produce his own labour force.

Our farm was like some vast apprenticeship school with skills and attitudes handed down from Father, the masterman at the top. From each according to his ability was the unwritten rule, and ability was measured by age. Between the ages of five and eighteen, I graduated in every task a grazier's farm throws up, from 'spudding' thistles and 'knocking' muck to making hayricks and calving cows. Those of us of school age made our contribution to work in the evenings, at week-ends and during holidays. Fortunately my regular schooling was not interfered with. My older brothers were not so lucky. When in later years I searched the primary school records, there seemed an all-too-obvious liaison between the local school headmaster and my father, who were friends, and it showed in the absences of my brothers at harvest time.

Until I was ten, the whole family was still under one roof. But like all large families, ours developed its subgroups based largely on age and shared experience. At

Our school in the next-door village of Church Langton

Tur Langton Manor, 'tucked away at the bottom of the village and approached by an elm-flanked drive'. *Photo: National Monuments Record*

Two village
landmarks, the
Forge and the
Chapel

the top of the pyramid were Robert, Muriel and Eric, remote and sometimes awesome. Robert was our hero. After surviving trench warfare in World War I he had returned home. He could shoot a rabbit on the run, throw a bullock, or shear a sheep in six minutes. He could whistle so loudly with four fingers in his mouth that your ears sang for minutes after. He owned a dress suit and a motorbike and had black curly hair. He attended week-end dances and was sought by every farmer's daughter for miles around, so pleasure was not entirely forgone. Since remote village dances often continued until one in the morning and you still had to see your partner home, Robert recalls that after a couple of hours in bed he was under the cows again to finish milking some by five a.m. and have milk in the town by six a.m. to secure an extra bonus of a penny a gallon. His expertise soon secured him a farm of his own and he has farmed ever since.

Muriel was a 'stunner' for looks and knew it. She also loved authority, and had plenty of chances to develop her skills with us younger ones. She read our minds before we knew them ourselves, and chastised us verbally for what she thought we might do. Being young herself, she knew our weaknesses, like failing to wash our feet, spending a penny when a halfpenny would do, shoetoeing the cat, firing airgun pellets through the cockerel's tail and calling girls we disliked 'bitches'. We liked her succession of farmer-suitors, for that often meant mince pies for supper and they often disbursed shillings on arrival. In return we kept clear of the drawing room, washed our faces specially well, and reported the first signs of the visitor's arrival, so that Muriel could appear with the necessary nonchalance as the visitor entered the drive. She had a quicksilver mind and had the farm not engulfed her would certainly have enjoyed an academic career. Inevitably social contacts were mainly with the farming community and she married into the ancient family of Kendall. Today, a widow, she still manages a large estate.

Eric had an entrepreneurial mind and farming had little appeal. Father scarcely understood his discontents though Mother gave secret support. The upshot was that he escaped the compelling family tradition and emigrated to New Zealand, soon to be joined by Douglas. Here his keen business instinct came to the fore and today, retired and rich, he indulges his taste for Maori art and carving.

In the middle family group were Douglas, Stanley and Vera. With the first two I had little rapport and I found them unpredictable: not old or wise enough to be respected, nor young enough to share my interests. Vera was different, being gentle, sensitive and sympathetic: perhaps she sensed that I, like her, did not have farming 'in my bones'. She was beautiful too and clearly marked by Nature for other than the farm kitchen. After grammar school she began a successful career as a model with a fashion house in Leicester. Then tragedy struck. She died of pneumonia with complications arising, said the doctor, from tuberculosis possibly bovine in origin. Such bitter irony affected us all. That was the only time I saw my father cry; not at the funeral, but out in the fields afterwards. And I wept with him.

At the bottom of the family pile were myself, Cecil and Dick. It was with Cecil that I found most common ground, and until I was eighteen, we were close companions. We slept, ate, played and worked together. We confided our inmost thoughts and gave mutual support when the adult world seemed to oppress. Many were our joint escapades. When I fell into a pond trying to reach moorhen's eggs Cecil, though half my size, pulled me out. One winter he knocked his front teeth out while sliding on ice, and I led him home with the bits of teeth in my pocket. Years later, on joining the RAF aged sixteen, that damage was the only fault in his medical record though he does recall how the doctors gathered round to see the boy with such unusual muscles on his shoulders. It was the end of haytime when he joined.

As for Dick, he was our shadow: sometimes irrelevant, occasionally a nuisance. Yet in retrospect I see that he came through to manhood remarkably well considering he was the youngest of nine. Dick loved agriculture and machinery, farming in England and later New Zealand. How ironic that his death, the second great family tragedy, should be caused by a tractor which rolled over, killing both him and his daughter.

Mother came out of Lincolnshire, her father being Robert Kingston, born 1815 in the year of Waterloo. He farmed near Pinchbeck, above Spalding, was also a surveyor, and contracted to supply Lincolnshire roads with granite from Leicestershire. Ethel, my mother, accompanied her father on one trip, and so met my father. He was not only farming, but handling granite for road metalling in Leicestershire.

Mother was certainly used to large families. Her father had six children by his first marriage and seven by his second. Mother came of the second brood. She was reared in a strong nonconformist tradition and her father built at his own expense a United Free Methodist Chapel. But Mother sickened of a stern religious up-bringing. I never recall her entering a chapel and she regarded the Anglican church as social ornament. Nevertheless she retained a strong puritanical streak and would certainly have agreed that 'to work is to pray'.

The Mother of my childhood was a tall, willowy, whip-lash figure. She manoeuvred around the kitchen so quickly that her arms and legs seemed often to have different intentions. Her hand could reach left for a cup while her body moved right to a saucer. She would simultaneously stir the fire and look into a boiling sauce-pan, or lift the kettle from the hob with one hand, and the tea from a shelf with the other. Whatever was next to be done was forever treading on the heels of what was not quite finished. She was restlessness personified, darting round the house under a grey cloud of hair from which streamed a meteor trail of fine white wisps and often a fall-out of hairpins. Whether she sat or stood, her starched apron whispered uneasily, like the first faltering winds before a storm. There was always the threat of demonic activity about her person, and I could rarely relax in her presence. Even when reading a newspaper she constantly plucked at the pages, beat them into a dozen shapes, folded and refolded the sheets. Yet she read fast, loved reading and week-long devoured the papers.

Her mind was as electric as her body. From the moment she rose in the morning, she sprayed orders far and wide: verbal injections to stir the mind, stimulate the body and prod the will. Domestic daily helpers and the family must be thrust into orbits that fitted her master plan for the day. From the kitchen command centre, messages would flow to the limits of house and farmyard. A call that breakfast would be ten minutes early could be shouted through the kitchen window, echoed by those in the drive, noised on through the farmyard and relayed to Father in the first meadow. Or a message 'not to take all day about it' could go via dining room, to stairs and bedroom, and finally to someone collecting cooking apples in the gloom of the far attic. A family of eleven plus other helpers constituted a ready-made chain of command. Laggards abed, myself included, received direct commands through the kitchen ceiling. Such broadsides could be followed by a grapeshot of detail by which we judged the mood of the day. Mother had a volatile temper; if she had a great head of steam, it must out. Orders, complaints and corrections would punctuate breakfast and spill over later to the postman and the cat. Mother's coal-black eyes burned deep as her words and no one was ever known to contradict her. Even salesmen whose call broke into morning routine were likely to receive sharp reproof. But knowing Mother and keen to take orders for cattle food, they suffered in silence. They knew too that her temper alternated with startling generosity and likely as not, they finished by the kitchen fire, taking tea and rock cakes and nursing the cat, which returned when it sensed the changing scene. And if they talked of their wives and families they usually left with a bonus of new-laid eggs. Whenever we boys fell foul of Mother, the quickest way back to grace was to find a windfall of eggs. So in winter we scoured the barns and hay stacks, in summer the ditches, nettlebeds and wood-piles. Failing eggs, a rabbit would do, so off to the hedge-rows with Nipper the terrier, and a ferret to put down the holes.

FATHER was proud of his grazier title. 'Better a man of grass than a man of straw,' he would joke. Shoulder high to a bullock, ankle deep in grass, was the vision of himself that he liked best. Grass dominated his life. Without good grass at the right time, cattle and sheep would not be 'good doers', milk yields would fall, breeding sheep would mother fewer and poorer lambs, hay yields would be light. The corollary of this, preached like a commandment, to all who would listen, was 'Good grass needs good muck.' A large, well-rotted muckheap, ripe and solid like peat, and ready for spreading on the fields, always roused Father's interest even when on someone else's land. On one rare occasion, Father took time off from work to drive Mother in a trap into Lincolnshire to visit relatives. When later I asked Mother how far it was, she replied after some hesitation, 'Two hundred muck-heaps and a lot of grass.' Mother's interests beyond those of housewife embraced travel, music, reading and con-versation with those outside the farming world. Raising nine children in such a grassy world as ours often proved exasperating and Mother would 'let fly' at Father for being so single-minded about work. When I left home at eighteen to study history at University, Father had only a grudging respect for my academic work. He changed remarkably when I investigated the family tree and dis-

covered that for centuries the Cramps had farmed the
heathlands and pastures near Charnwood Forest. He
would have been delighted had he lived to know of my
discovery that a certain Job Cramp's will in the eighteenth
century showed that he left his heir 'the mighty dunghill
in the cowclose', to say nothing of 'half a bull' which
served the cows of himself and a neighbour.

Father hated writing. Before he signed cheques, the
recipient had to complete the details. He kept all the
records he considered essential in one small dog-eared
diary in his waistcoat pocket. Entries were mainly of
wages, purchases of animal foods and animals, sales of
stock and hay, calving dates of cows entered by their
name, dates when sheep were put to the ram, and the
number of cattle and sheep in particular fields. No trades-
man, salesman or merchant was ever paid unless he
applied to Father in person, either at home or in the
cattle market. This enabled Father to ignore all bills
coming by post which were simply stored on their edges,
unopened, in old cardboard boxes. Father's only reading
was *The Farmer and Stockbreeder*, which he perused
in the kitchen with his early morning cup of tea at six
o'clock.

Father's policy for successful farming followed certain
simple formulae. As regards cattle and sheep, 'Buy well
and they're half sold' was the maxim. Of the milking
cows he said, 'Fill the cows and they'll fill the churns.' He
certainly gave great attention to their diet. But the over-
riding commandment was, 'Work hard, pay out as little
as you must, and profit and pleasure will be the result.' He
did not always phrase the latter point quite like that; he
sometimes said, 'You will avoid loss.' The result of this
philosophy was work from dawn to dusk and beyond.
Although we younger members of the family occasionally
escaped to play football or cricket with local boys — in
the field of another farmer, of course — Father tried to
shame us out of 'chasing a bit of leather with a lot of

hooligans'. When an ex-army captain tried to start a
Scout troop in the village, Father was positively alarmed;
said he could teach us all the tracking we needed in finding
stray sheep; and teach us all the knots we were likely to
want, when we loaded wagons and harnessed horses. In
the finish, in an unprecedented moment of generosity, he
gave Cecil and me tuppence each not to attend the in-
augural Scout meeting. When we heard next day that the
Scout plan had been abandoned, we spent the money
quickly in case Father asked for it back.

Not only did work dominate the life of the family, but
laughter and sentiment were considered alien to this purpose. The ant not the grasshopper was our model. There
was no talk of ghosts round our kitchen fire when the north-
east wind howled in the chimney on a winter's night. We
were left in no doubt that out there in the gale were cattle
and sheep — that was all! And they would need a specially
early foddering after such a rough night. The rattling
chains and eerie squeaks that came out of the winter
darkness were the gate you forgot to hasp; and that
hideous shadow in the drive was a calf escaped from its
pen. In our practical world superstition had no place: it
could easily be an excuse to avoid work. No notice was
ever taken of birthdays, and presents were never ex-
changed except at Christmas. Parties Father referred to as
'junketings' or 'bun struggles'. For him they spelt expense,
wasted time and harmful food like bloater paste sandwiches, fizzy drinks and coloured jellies. His stern view
of the latter stemmed from the knowledge that the stinking bones processed by a local glue factory yielded by-
products which went into jellies.

Waste of any kind was frowned on and I opened my
eyes daily to a fretwork carving on my bedroom wall
spelling out, 'Waste not want not'. If Mother considered
any of us had spent money unnecessarily she accused us of
'eating our white bread first'. It seems the Lincolnshire
labourers of her childhood had often to be content with

dark home-made rye-bread, and the white wheaten loaf was a treat. In our house, nothing was renewed or replaced unless absolutely necessary. Table knives were sharpened and ground down till some resembled daggers. The clock on the mantelpiece only worked with a wad of paper under one side, but it worked. Draughts blew under the kitchen door, but it was said to make the fire burn better, so nothing was done to stop it. When sheets and blankets became holed they were turned sides to middle. When that no longer sufficed, they became bandages, flannels, dusters, and polishers, all carefully hemmed. Personal clothes were handed down from child to child, and I never remember wearing new clothes till I went to Grammar School. Egg shells and broken pottery were pulverised to provide grit for the hens. Goose grease was preserved to rub on the chest against winter coughs, and anoint hands and toes when we had chilblains. All string was husbanded and knots carefully undone. Water buckets with holes became coal buckets; broken metal handles were replaced with cord. Brooms were used down to the last whisker and then used for firewood. Meat bones were hoarded for the rag-and-bone man after the dog had had his picking. When boots finally wore out, tongues and tops were removed to repair harness. Rabbit skins were dried and preserved to make gloves. Household waste went to the pigs. The hens drank their water from chamber pots which had lost their handles. When we killed hens, the soft feathers were used to re-stuff pillows. By such means were 'outgoings' reduced.

I once heard Father say, 'There's one good thing about being a farmer: nobody can set up in opposition.' I understood his point. No man is so much a king as a farmer standing in the midst of the acres he owns; few men can feel so much in control of their destiny. Reality for Father was his farm and his work; all else were adjuncts. Mother provided food and bed, we children provided labour in our several ways. But we were only 'somebody' in so far as we contributed to the central cause. When our interests, hopes and plans deviated from this, Father was usually indifferent. When two older brothers planned to emigrate, Father offered neither aid nor obstacle. They had become irrelevant. The back of a bullock under Father's hand had more real meaning than our own heads. He registered more outward concern about the nutrition of his cows than about our own diet. The comforts of home received no comment; the stalls of the cows were a matter for daily concern. Mother said more than once that Father's affection went in and out at his feet, for the earth was his first and lasting love.

In dealings with his own kind, however, Father was at his most vital. Thus, having made up his mind, say, to sell some fat cattle, he would plan the sale with all the tactical care of a general about to do battle. He preferred to sell bullocks in the field where they grazed, rather than suffer the hazards of a sale ring. A week before offering for sale, they were fed extra well, to 'bulk them up'. Then, just before the prospective purchaser arrived, the hair along their back was teased up with a stiff brush to give a square look to the hindquarters where the best meat lies. For the *denouement*, the cattle were sold if possible with the declining sun behind them to make them look larger than life. Of course the purchaser had his gambits too. He would try to 'crab' the animals, point out poor features imaginary or real, and use the appropriate language to reinforce his point. 'That b ... ought to be back on mother's milk, he's so small.' Or, if the cattle were dirty through wintering in a shed, 'Take the head, horns and guts away, and the shit off his flanks, and what's left?'

If Father stressed size, the buyer wanted quality; if Father mentioned quality, the buyer would say, 'But don't forget the butcher's income stops when the scales stop turning.' At some stage, if Father stuck to his price, the buyer would hint that he had another farm to visit, and would try the walking-away ploy. A pace or two ahead of Father, he would head for the pony and trap, slapping his leggings with his walking stick to emphasise he would not raise his offer. Trotting home with Father, they would talk about the weather and other inconsequential details. But all was not lost. 'Better meet the wife and have a drink.' So into the kitchen, where sooner or later, over whisky or beer, cattle again entered the conversation, or Mother, sensing impasse, would deftly raise the topic. In the final phase, there was much talk of 'meeting half way' on the price, till finally, as in an Indian market, the deal was done. There followed a symbolic spitting on right hands, which were smacked firmly together: a sort of ritual mixing of 'blood', a holy rite after which there was no going back. But there still remained the final act of blessing. The buyer claimed, and received, 'luck money'. One or two pounds in cash were pressed into his palm, to correct the scales of justice to the last pennyweight.

Three episodes illustrate how significant were animals to Father, and how farming lay at the heart of his being. I was the last of the family to marry, and it was agreed that, although I was living away from home, I should be married from the farmhouse where Mother and Father still lived. It was early April, and lambing time. One hour before we were all due in church five miles away, Father was still with his lambing ewes. While I paced around the kitchen awaiting him, I decided that now of all times merited a drink. I was in the act of pouring out some brandy for Mother, the best man and myself, when Father entered the kitchen with two starved lambs. His only remark was, 'Steady on with the brandy, or there won't be enough for the lambs.' We only just arrived at church in time, in a car that had a distinct smell of the farmyard, combined with that from anti-fox oil, an evil-smelling deterrent daubed on newborn lambs. During the journey I was worried by loud bumps from the rear of the car and I feared for the springs. Only later did I learn that the noise came from Trimmer, the sheepdog. Father had shut him in the boot, so that after the wedding reception he could proceed directly to the evening shepherding.

On a sad occasion, at a time when Mother lay ill in bed downstairs, Father bought a prize ram at the sheep fair. As usual in such cases, the animal was beautifully groomed, had a back like a table, and was completely docile. Father told the housekeeper to prepare tea on a tray. This he placed on the ram's back, and led the beribboned animal down the ground floor corridor to Mother's room, till it stood alongside her bed. Mother delighted in the whole episode and patted the ram appreciatively. It must be a record of some sort. The housekeeper was not so pleased when the ram left a watery trail on his return journey. Father's jesting response was, 'No rams, no lambs.'

In a way, the third episode complements the second. Father had been to market one Tuesday, as usual, and sadly was hit by a car as he left on foot. He sustained a broken leg, was hospitalised and came home with his leg in plaster. He was eighty-eight years old, but we all thought he was on the way to complete recovery. About this time, a load of bullocks for fattening arrived at the home farm from Wales. We immediately had them detained in the yard and asked Father if we could push his bed to the window to see them. His answer was quiet and deliberate. 'Take them to the field: I don't want to see them.' Nor did he. I reported the episode to the family doctor, who alerted us that Father had probably decided he had seen enough of life. A week later he was dead.

The Village Stage

THE PAST died gracefully in Langton. Like the old folks, it tended to shrivel, to withdraw to quiet places, and make its final bow so quietly that the passing was scarcely noticed. Thus the main social structure seemed eternal. There were some small changes that touched my boyhood. Men came with a fiery furnace and tarred the main street, and robbed us of puddles of pleasure. Father said that horses would now break their necks. Cars appeared, with magic names — Trojan, Clyno, De Dion Bouton, Singer and Ford. We collected their numbers on the backs of old envelopes and swapped them, or bartered them for 'fag cards'. Piped water came and 'unfit for drinking' appeared on pumps whose water had nourished us for generations. Some young men vanished forever to Canada and Australia, seeking a better life, though how, no one in our village could imagine. Stud stallions were based in our village and taken for a walk every day. I watched from a safe distance the first confrontation of one with a tractor. Boys stopped wearing celluloid collars and one or two women smoked 'fags' on the quiet. A rich 'towny' rented a village property and commuted daily to his factory in Leicester — by car!

But life in Langton was still largely based on a rural economy. Landowner, labourer and village craftsman still formed the heart of the community, and men looked back to the ways and values of their forebears as readily as they looked to the future. We still had a lord of the manor, in practice if not in name. He lived at the Manor House, tucked away at the bottom of the village and approached by an elm-flanked drive. He also had the biggest farm, employed most labour, and was a magistrate. Boys called him 'Sir', and touched their caps, girls curtsied when he strolled through the village, tweedily clad, shotgun under his arm. I had mixed views about his farming; being rich, he could farm as a hobby and still survive. What an extravagance, I thought, to have all his farm gates painted white and adorned with his initials. And what luxury, to have Jacob sheep and Highland cattle in his home meadow, just for show, and never a cow on his whole six hundred acres. But I held it in his favour that, sitting as a Justice, he was hard on poachers, arson and attacks on property.

Those who ventured down the manor drive in summertime were always impressed (provided they were not farmers) by scores of over-fat Hereford bullocks seeking the shade of the elms, and awaiting the admiration of county socialites who attended the manor's tennis parties. These cattle were destined to sweep the board at the local fatstock show. A week after this event their carcasses, still sporting rosettes, would hang in the shops of local butchers.

The lady of the manor was a shrewish woman. It was said that both the money and the brains behind the farm organisation were hers. She rode to hounds every week during the season, and broke her collar-bone every winter. She rode sidesaddle. According to her groom it was an unnecessary precaution, since long ago she had lost that which the sidesaddle habit was intended to preserve. She terrorised the workmen by appearing suddenly on horseback in the most remote parts of the farm. Those who went to sleep on the job were likely to be awakened with a horsewhip.

There were two attractive daughters of marriageable age. Left to themselves the girls would undoubtedly have found suitable husbands. But mother was determined to arrange their future, and interpreted the term 'marriage market' literally. Having first built an addition to the manor to act as a ballroom (locals called it the mousetrap), she began arranging parties. It was said that she had drawn up a shortlist of twenty possible husbands. Mother's next ploy was to have farm pupils from 'good families'. Comfortably housed in the village, she regarded them either as tame escorts, or as potential suitors in their own right. However, the daughters not only inherited mother's vitality but superior wisdom too. One found her own way to marriage, family and fortune. The other with equal determination chose spinsterhood. Then with one of fate's bitter ironies tragedy struck. Their father died in a shooting accident. Since the only son had died earlier in a motor cycle accident the manor estate had perforce to be sold: 'given away' said my Father, since land values were at rock bottom. The outcome was that the mother found solace with her unmarried daughter in a former labourer's cottage.

Of rather less consequence than the people at the manor were two or three gentleman farmers; but they farmed badly and were glad on occasions to seek Father's advice. 'If they were sold up, the banks would need most of it,' he remarked, and in one case was right.

As owner-farmers, our closest ties were with families like ourselves. If work meant salvation, we were all amongst the Elect; if muck meant money, we were solvent. We viewed gentleman farmers with polite indifference; they were knights in armour, protected from the main battle dangers; profligate with their own kind, mean to their employees, and as the twenties progressed, often financially overstretched. As for ourselves, we thought we had the balance of life just right. We nurtured too a sense of history. I knew land gave status, but for me it had also a spiritual quality. It gave a man roots; he was linked by the soil to his ancestors, and he planned for generations to come; he had a stake in eternity. God made heaven and earth; if you owned a bit of the latter, it seemed to bring a slice of heaven with it. Land, animals, crops, wagons: they all gave a sense of security, belonging and purpose; and though I found few words to speak my thoughts, I knew the family shared them. Never for us a morning awakening and wondering what to do, for the land was there — always. Always the land and the seasons and the work; the pace of the horse and the plough and the wagon; the company of the sun, and the frost and the rain. I was part of Nature's rhythmic dance and would live for ever and ever — like Father. It seemed impossible he could die; it followed that I was eternal.

I don't suppose the Vicar would have agreed. He served all five Langtons and our village was only a chapelry. However, it managed one service every Sunday, and two at Christmas and Easter. All members of our family knew they were Church of England and Tory: no one ever debated the fact, which seemed part of the natural order of things. So much so that attending church or political meetings seemed almost superfluous to my young mind. We were already the converted and only an occasional nod in the direction of God and the King was considered necessary. We met our MP every four or five years at election time, and we young ones were members of the Junior Imperial and Constitutional League. We met God when compelled to Sunday school, and at every Christmas and Harvest Festival. If God could have arranged it with Father to muck the cows out and do shepherding on Sunday, things might have been different. Nor did our indifferent church going upset the Vicar. He always timed his visits for Saturday morning, when Mother's big cook took place, and he sampled freely. As for the MP, he knew where we were; he hunted over our land and we could call on both him and God in emergency.

The Vicar was an Oxford graduate and completely lacked the common touch. His lifestyle in an Adam rectory left him insulated from the majority of his parishioners, and his visits were mainly to people of substance. When he became a canon, I longed to ask him what he had done to deserve the honour, but I lacked the maturity and courage. When he gained his Doctorate of Music he was at great pains to inform as many as could understand that he wished henceforth to be addressed as 'Doctor ——'. For a clergyman to place the academic honour before the ecclesiastical, again seemed odd to my young mind. And how could such a learned man sermonise for half an hour on the difficulty of a camel getting through a needle's eye, in order to show the odds against the rich entering heaven? It seemed to me that he accepted his own chances without qualms. And if he had a real problem, there were plenty of poor folk ready to help him solve it.

Small wonder that congregations were usually in single figures and frequently consisted of bellringer, organ blower, organist and one or two others. The Vicar's great love was music; he persuaded the old inhabitants to sing the ditties and folk songs they remembered from their childhood and he set them down to music. This is probably his best memorial.

My closest contact with the Vicar came when attending confirmation classes at the rectory with other village children. We learned the catechism by heart, though our questions were never invited. As a farmer's son, I was impressed with the response which enjoined '. . . not to covet or desire other men's goods . . . and to do my duty in that state of life unto which it shall please God to call me'. For my two companions were labourers' children and the father of one was unemployed. How could one be content with little or nothing in the midst of plenty, I wondered, and for one of the rare times in my early life, I felt uncomfortable in the presence of other children. Curiously, I counted it in the Vicar's favour, that his study was barny and cold; though not as cold as the vicarage in a neighbouring village, where the rector lived in a tent pitched in his drawing room and facing the fire.

Ironically our lives were considerably enriched as the result of the ambitions of an eccentric eighteenth-century predecessor of the Vicar. In 1749 the Rev. William Hanbury entered upon the living of Church Langton though he too had 'care of souls' for all five Langtons. In an age of charitable foundations Hanbury wanted to excel them all. He planned charitable trusts to establish at Church Langton a Collegiate Educational Centre on Oxford College lines with a magnificent minster, picture gallery, printing press, library, grammar school, hospital and alms houses. To fund his enterprises he planned music festivals and promoted in his parish church a performance of Handel's *Messiah*. But the more ambitious fund raiser revealed in his *Essay on Planting* was to grow trees by the million and sell off both young trees and mature timber, investing the proceeds at compound interest. Sadly his ambitions proved too challenging for his trustees and after his death only watered-down schemes survived.

Nevertheless the endowments he left have had a lasting influence on our village life. They have provided education for all village children since 1860, while scholarships to grammar school and university from which I benefited, were added later. Our own old and ruinous church was demolished and a new one built. Trust funds also provided for the sick in our community both in their homes and in hospital. Since the eighteenth century villagers have had access to a free lending library and until modern times free beef at Christmas was distributed to all needy folk.

Time and the Welfare State have clouded the significance of William Hanbury's work. But when I was a boy there was not a family in Tur Langton who could not benefit in mind, body, or estate from the work of this practical visionary.

FATHER, who never carried a penny piece on his person, gloried in his rough working clothes: a patched jacket, breeches, leggings and heavy boots. 'A bit of honest muck never hurt anybody,' he would say, but with the conviction of a man who had a warm hearth, home-cured ham and a change of clothes waiting for him at the end of the day. As for me, I never felt more proud than riding home through the village on top of a laden hay wagon pulled by two horses. If a small boy shouted 'Cocksy bugger' and rushed indoors, I enjoyed it all the more. From my vantage point I could look down on the upturned faces of women and children or glance into skimpily curtained cottage bedrooms, glimpsing iron bedsteads, spread with patchwork quilts, and wallpaper gay with sprays of flowers that seemed to fill the tiny rooms. Sometimes I traversed the village on horseback, or light trap, but always on business bent. More often I was leading a cartload of hay, straw or manure, walking belly high to a sweating horse, and threatened by rumbling wheels behind me and iron clad hooves at my side.

Seeming to fall into a group of their own were the craftsmen and those rendering personal service. The carpenter Zach Busby, with whimsical humour, said he catered for the quick and the dead, for he was also wheelwright and undertaker. The blacksmith Bill Rogers could shoe a shire horse or a hunter, make a child's hoop or a shelf bracket. His smithy was a source of live entertainment, with the chance of a bonus of 'hossmuck' if you volunteered to pump the forge bellows. One or two smallholders with a few rented fields were proud to have escaped the common ruck. With monies saved from piecework thatching and hedgecutting, they strove towards a freehold heaven. Few loved our police sergeant; he was troublesome as a conscience, too often popping up at the wrong time. Our post office was like a confessional, and the postmistress was better informed on our misdoings than the parson. The two publicans were the poor man's priests. They did most business on Sundays and kept a little bit of heaven in their cellars.

Labourers formed our most numerous class. A few

worked in factories in local towns; most loved the outdoor life and drifted onto the land straight from school. 'Our man', as we always called him, was typical of his class. Other than work, their chief interests were the pub, the allotment, and bed, and they bred mightily. Most wore corduroy trousers, hitched below the knee; this kept the bottoms free of mud and preserved body warmth. The trousers were supported by a wide leather belt, riding low over the belly. This served the dual purpose of preventing hernias and displaying badges and buttons from the Great War. They smoked 'Woodbines', the poor man's cigarette, bought in flimsy packets of five. Some old men chewed 'twist' and developed a great facility at spitting a jet of thin brown fluid six feet ahead of them. Lunch in the field was a cottage loaf with cheese or boiled fat bacon injected between top and bottom. This was supplemented by a bottle of cold sweet tea.

The Great War scratched at our calm for a time; Father made some profit from grazing remount horses for the cavalry and supplying fodder. Several villagers fought and survived; six did not, and we carved their names in granite. For a year or two after 1918, ex-Servicemen at the Christmas concert sang 'When the Roll is called up yonder I'll be there'. Villagers subscribed to buy an army hut and called it the Village Hall. Farmers who had been forced to plough up fields rapidly put them down to grass again. Only one radical worker muttered about his rights, and that usually when well laced with ale. His son had been wounded, had recovered and returned safely, but his father, with rare alliteration, lamented, 'The plutty Prussians nigh killed our Perce. The puggers put a payonet in his paunch and he can't touch a decent bit of fat meat now. Time the plutty government gi'ed him a penshun.' But this was a lone voice and 'our Perce' still managed to work, thrive and drink his quota of beer.

Most people still found satisfaction in the inter-dependence of village life and had respect for the varied talents of those who composed it. Smith might be a loud mouth after a few drinks on Saturday night, but he could layer a hedge better than most. The roadman might poach a few rabbits and curse newfangled cars, but he kept the drains open, and gritted the roads well in winter. The midwife and the baker were everybody's friends. The farms gave employment, and much that the townsman paid dearly for: firewood, garden manure, fresh straw for mattresses, cheap potatoes, turnips, eggs and milk. Tied cottage rents were nominal and our man had free milk and potatoes. Every labourer had an allotment. Enterprising wives would salt runner beans, pickle onions, make blackberry jam and feed a few hens on household waste. Some knew how to make do with a large piece of brisket, a sheep's head or hocks bought cheaply in the markets at nine o'clock on Saturday night when the stalls closed. Most cottages were never without a large bowl of dripping to spread on toast. The labourer's wife often helped in the farm kitchen and, besides being paid, often went home 'with a bit'a summat under the apron' given by the farmer's wife.

Some labouring families had been in the village for generations. There were also feckless ones, who wandered from farm to farm leaving a trail of debt, with the baker always the chief victim. But most labourers took a near-proprietary interest in their surroundings. They knew the owner of every field, its name and acreage. They knew where to find the best blackberries, mushrooms and hazelnuts. After a stormy night they were first up, gathering fallen wood. I would see them on summer evenings, following the streams, collecting teazels, moor-hens' eggs, watercress and driftwood. If they saw sheep 'cast' on their backs, they pulled them upright. If un-savoury tramps were wandering about our fields, we were soon informed.

With bus services sporadic, and the railway station two miles away, our closed community was given to much gossip and privacy outside your own house was difficult to come by. Any departure from normal routine was a matter for immediate comment by those with little else to excite their day.

'Nine o'clock and the postman's still at Maggie Carter's house. What's so special about her cups of tea?'

Or, 'Fancy postman calling on her! They say she writes letters to herself to get him to call.'

The true countryman is more longsighted than his town cousin. He can identify others by their silhouette, gait, speed and direction of movement. 'There's old Joe off to the allotment. Bit early for him though. And where's young Bill going? Too early for courting or poaching.'

But the harshest criticisms were levelled by poorer folk at those of their own kind who seemed to be getting 'uppity'. 'Who does Fanny Grant think she is, entering for a beauty competition? Ought to have red hair, she had. And that Bill Garner. Just lashed out and bought a new suit. Started drinking pints instead of halves too. Soon won't know which side his arse hangs.'

When one married farmer started to attend chapel and take a deep interest in the Sunday school and its lady teacher, it provided some fine ammunition for the Anglicans. But the tables were turned when the Vicar fell ill and we had a young curate. In quick time the choir had more sopranos than ever before. 'Choir practice, indeed! That Mary Goodman with a plungeline dress, mincing into church like a cat on hot bricks as soon as the first clang of the bell sounds. And that Molly Hare. She's got two strings to her bow already. But you know what they say — if one isn't enough, a dozen isn't too many. Then there's that red-headed Maggie Holmes with a voice like a corncrake and not a note of music in her head. They say she held the book of psalms upside down last week. Ginger for pluck, I say, and sandy pigs for acorns, but I doubt whether her efforts will bear much fruit.' So the 'Chapelites' had their dig at the Established Church.

Then there was Patty Jones, a young widow, living in an isolated cottage. How did she manage to live anyway, unless with a little outside help? She couldn't dress as she did on a widow's pension. And why did half the footpaths in the village have side tracks finishing in the field near her house? 'And what of the Briggs girl; big as a house side again. Her mother says she's going away into service again next week. Had too much service already if you ask me; she'll be back in a few months, half the size and twice as natural. Wonder if mother will tell the same story as last time — came home because the job didn't suit her and she lost weight.'

More sinister rumours were linked with one woman who came from the city as housekeeper to a farmer and stayed on in the village after his death. It was said she could 'get girls out of trouble' if they went to her soon enough, or she could give them addresses in the city where they could get help. I doubt if many village girls availed themselves of her services. Babies born out of wedlock were either adopted or 'run in' with their grandmother's family.

Some village happenings were a nine days' wonder, like the case of the old farmer who took to the bottle. When he suffered DTs, a full-time nurse was called in to assist his housekeeper. For brief intervals he was 'dried out' but always relapsed, bribing his gardener to conceal whisky in his hen house or stables. Beyond these places he became too weak to venture. But earlier on he must have had his little caches of whisky well dispersed. Village lads discovered two; one in the base of a rotten elm tree, another in an abandoned barn under a bucket among some rubbish. There's probably some good vintage stuff still to be found, but our friend will not enjoy it. He died of gangrene in both legs.

Sometimes it seemed that our village needed moments of madness, in order to establish the relevance of sanity. Such moments seemed to come when boredom crushed the normal zest for life, and families sought relief in minor bickerings amongst themselves. One family would complain that a neighbour's dog had fouled their doorstep; or they had placed a stinking rabbit hutch near their back door; or 'someone' was stealing the soft water from the water butt at the side of the house. Occasionally the quarrels took on a personal note. 'Don't your Mary go saying our Madge was sent home from school because she had nits in her hair. I do my kids' heads with quassia chips every week.' Or 'Don't think because your Joe's left school and bringing home a bit a money you can get stuck up and put on airs and graces.' Only once did I hear of real battle done — hatpins and all! But such tiffs were of short duration and would suddenly vanish when people were reminded that real tragedy could strike. Then they seemed to close ranks in a wave of outgoing sympathy. Take the case of Job Ingram. He was such a quiet fellow, and a bit on the slow side, but liked by everyone. He cycled daily four miles to the glue factory and worked amid its stench uncomplainingly. He shovelled bones with a will and sometimes worked with his feet in a sea of maggots. Could such a man have a girlfriend who would meet him straight out of work, and love him unkempt and unwashed as he was? Well, to everyone's surprise, Job did, and she was a good honest girl too. Then one winter evening she met Job to 'call it off'. He lived with his widowed mother, and wouldn't marry while she was alive, and Nelly wouldn't wait any longer. Job's answer was swift and sure. He slashed both wrists with the pocket knife he used to carve his lunch with. When searchers from the village found him, it was too late.

Such incidents set everybody's conscience tingling. Job's funeral filled the church. Folks were saying they really wished they'd talked to Job a bit more and realised he could both love and be loved.

*

IN COURSE OF TIME, Saturday dances in our village hall became quite popular. Rich and poor, villager and townsman, rubbed shoulders in the Valeta, the Barn dance, the Polka and the Lancers. At Christmas, extra special dances were arranged: special, because there were prizes for a 'spot waltz', for the best looking couple, and for the best set in the Lancers. The spot waltz seemed to go well enough, till the Master of Ceremonies, the only one who knew 'the spot', ordered the band to stop playing. The prize went to his daughter and her fiancé, amidst some subdued but muttered protest. It was a hand-knitted shawl. Some said she'd soon need it for a little stranger her father didn't know about. However, the evening proceeded to the dance for the best looking pair. The dancers circled the hall and three couples were eventually drawn out. They stood before the panel while everyone else took their seats. The panel consisted of a farmer, a retired gentleman and the barmaid from the 'top pub'. It was really a contest for the girls. The farmer had an eye for size and said so. He regarded the event as a sort of fatstock show. He argued the point loudly and plumped for a local lass with prominent breasts and buttocks. The gentleman took a more discerning view. He favoured 'a nifty little piece' from the neighbouring town, with thin legs, fully-fashioned stockings, high heels and, as my sister reported, 'breasts no larger than small apples'. The barmaid made yet a third choice for first prize, of a girl not unlike herself; good-looking in a coarse way, heavy with rouge and mascara, and a beauty spot on one cheek which she repeatedly dabbed in case it became dislodged.

It was clear that a consensus would never be reached, or, if it was, there would be ructions. So when one wag shouted, 'Draw lots,' the panel took refuge in the suggestion, pronouncing all the girls equally beautiful. The thin girl was drawn first. She paraded the hall on her partner's arm, amid appreciative stamping of feet that made the French chalk and dust so rise from the floor that few people were clearly visible below the knees.

But it was the Lancers that will live longest in village annals. The movements were gone through several times and the spirit of competition was keen amongst the sets. Finally, the leading set was chosen, this time by the Parson, who had looked in as always on the offchance of free refreshment. At his suggestion, the winning set gave a repeat performance. The band struck up; round and round, in and out, the dancers whirled, encouraged by the admiring crowd who stood or sat round the walls of the hall. The men in the set were husky and country bred, the women folk smaller and lighter. At every whirl the men displayed their strength, and the women, never before the centre of so much attraction, periodically lifted their feet as custom was and became airborne on the arms of the men. The whirl was repeated again and again till disaster struck. Poor Mrs Owen, though strong in the legs, was a trifle weak in the head, and amidst hysterical laughter she let go her arms. She spun away from the circling group at a tangent. Some said it was fifteen feet before she landed. At all events, so great was the impetus and so glossed the floor, that she slid the length of the hall. She passed under the refreshment table, scarcely disturbing the cloth which hung down. Guests at the end of the hall towards which she slid were too thunderstruck to act, possibly because the band continued to play. The unfortunate lady reached the end of her journey with her head and shoulders wedged under a chair, the occupant of which had lifted her legs in horror.

Brandy and smelling salts restored the victim. For years there was talk of her suing someone. But few villagers knew much about the law, and how could daft Lucy prove she had been made dafter by the accident? Old inhabitants still point to the spot on the wall where she came to rest.

Eat Well and Lie Warm

A T FIRST GLANCE our kitchen resembled the between-decks of a wooden battleship. It was wide and low and conveyed a sense of impending action. Dark oak beams, still bearing marks of the adze, caused tall men to stoop. Stone walls two feet thick were pierced with tiny windows. Breathtaking heat rolled across the kitchen from the red 'glee' of a fire six bars deep. When I was very young it seemed often out of control as flames clawed into the black void behind the chimney 'blower' and seemed to continue eternally up the chimney. Armies of sparks manoeuvred back and forth in the soot of the chimney mouth, flared briefly, and died. Occasionally, when new coals were added to the incandescent mass, meteor sparks hurled out in protest and the cat retreated from the hearth, leaving in his wake the smell of singeing fur. But I need not have feared; Mother was a master of fire in all its moods. Here at the centre of power, Mother strove to implement Father's dictum, 'Eat well and lie warm.'

Mother's first lieutenant was my eldest sister Muriel, while able-bodied village women made tactical appearances to attend to cutlery, sewing, dressmaking, and above all, cleaning. Farmhouse or not, Mother was strict on hygiene. Nothing upset her more than 'cowmuck traipsed onto the kitchen floor', a sheep tick found in a bed, or mice raiding the pantry while the house cat slept on the hearth only a few paces away. Normally the house shone, top to bottom; Father joked that his bureau was held together with polish, and even the cat slid on the lino.

Our house had two main storeys and attics in the roof. At ground level were four rooms and two cold pantries. The back kitchen served as coal store, wash-house and bathroom. Then in line down the length of the house came living kitchen, sitting room and drawing room. The sitting room was chiefly used at week-ends, for there was little sitting on other days, except in the kitchen in the evening. Here Mother and Father had cushioned armchairs and we children had elmwood railbacks. Our seats were so polished we either sat upright or slid onto the floor. The drawing room was a holy of holies, with gloomy wallpaper and a piano round which we sang hymns on Sunday evenings while Mother played. Upstairs were four large square bedrooms, where in Father's words you could 'get on with the business of sleeping'.

But the kitchen was hub of our universe, dominated by a shone black cooking range and the fire that threatened to burn through its ribs. The hobs were never free of saucepans and kettles, the kitchen never without the bouquet of the meal last eaten or the one in preparation. Along a second side of the kitchen was a vast sink, so deep we bathed in it till aged five, when we graduated to a round tin bath in the back kitchen. Fortunately for Mother, the sink lay under a window looking onto the main drive to the farmyard, so she kept in touch with activities. She could intercept strangers going up, hens wandering down, or outwit the Parson if he called too often.

A Welsh dresser filled a third side of the kitchen. Its hooks dripped with the history of a working day, for ornament, like sentiment, found little place in our house and our fine china was not displayed. Instead there were store keys, small household tools, spare lampwicks, candlesticks, enamelled mugs, bodkins for repairing sacks, receipts, the baker's bread book, police sheep-dipping memos, scissors and string. The dresser cupboards were largely filled with medicines and instruments for doctoring animals. The latter included tools for de-horning cattle, branding irons, syringes, 'drenching' cans for forcing medicines down animals' throats, 'bulldog' grips for holding animals by the nose, and rods for clearing animals' throats when potatoes became stuck. There were medicines for calving cows, scouring calves, horses with colic, dogs with worms, cattle with ringworm or husk. Occupying a much smaller space in the cupboard were family specifics, including Epsom salts. The first attack of any headache, stomach ache, or muscular ache was always treated with 'salts', administered in warm water for quick action. I hated this so much I learned to conceal my symptoms.

There was a distinct hierarchy in the family, based on age, for the older you were, the harder you worked and the higher you stood in the pecking order. This was reflected in the kitchen at meal times. We dined at a long, narrow, scrubbed-white, deal table which ran down the centre of the kitchen, reaching from the cooking range to the door leading into the yard. At the cosy end sat Father and Mother with their feet on a thick pegged rug. Farthest from food and fire, with backsides near the door, sat we lesser ones with our feet on lino if lucky, quarry tiles if not. Food for main meals was served piping hot, straight from hob, oven and pot, to table. Father did all the carving after a ritual knife-sharpening. As each plate was filled at the business end it was passed down to us younger ones who ate in silence. No remark was addressed to us save, perchance, a rebuke for scraping our plate over-loud, or for noisily drinking our broth, or 'wolfing' food without chewing it thoroughly.

Adult conversation was mainly on farming matters, and that meant the outlook was gloomy. There were no good days: they were 'pretty fair', bad or very bad. No matter how good the hay crop, the 'fall' of lambs, the number of heifer calves (for the dairy), the milk yield, no matter how good a purchase or a sale, no one in my hearing ever said so. My memories are of milk prices too low, tithes iniquitous, seasons too wet or too dry, and the price of fat cattle, sheep and wool so low that I imagined disaster lurked round the corner — until I discovered the truth.

Farmers have a perverse philosophy: trouble or its prospect make delightful conversation when you know that
you're basically safe. So pretend that you don't know
winters are cold and sheep sometimes die, and summers
are hot and ponds dry up. Pretend you are daily surprised
at these perils, for to accept that you know is to lose the
illusion of daily avoiding disaster. So perhaps Father's
pleasure was secretly to know that the world would be
daily surprised that the eleven Cramps not only survived
but, against all the odds, prospered.

TUESDAY had a special magic for me, when at four
o'clock Mother and Father arrived home from market
and unloaded the groceries from the high trap. Into the
kitchen came a smell spicy as an Indian market. No sterile
pre-packed food in plastic bags, but provisions selected by
Mother like a connoisseur: cheese she had 'tasted', tea to
her own blending, dates in large lumps carved from an
even bigger block on the grocer's counter. I sniffed and
guessed at the contents of the dark blue bags of rice, sago,
spices, sultanas and other wonders. Out came biscuits in
seven-pound tins, custard powder, candles, lampwicks,
and elastic for garters and bloomers: packet after packet!
Surely we should never want for anything again, and
when I carried the empty cartons to the back kitchen, I
poked my head into every one for a final breath of the
wonders they once held.

Though many of our needs were satisfied from our farm
and garden, we were never allowed to forget that what we
consumed of eggs and milk meant less to sell. We ate
whatever was put in front of us: 'fads and fancies' were
not allowed. During several months of the year, cows were
calving, so we had 'beestings', the first rich 'milk' after
calving, which bakes to an excellent custard. When
autumn-threshed wheat was available, Mother boiled it
in a cloth in a large iron pot. This 'frumerty' was served

with treacle and butter. In autumn we shot young pigeons and rooks for pies, and since no plough had disturbed our land for centuries, mushrooms were abundant. The village had several walnut trees; we purchased and pickled the fruit. True to her Lincolnshire origins, Mother loved fish, so Tuesday tea included steamed cod. Mother, however, ate crab or prawns, often with pickled samphire seaweed.

Saturday was the day of the big cook, when for three hours after breakfast no man dared set foot in the kitchen. Between nine o'clock and twelve, sufficient food was cooked, not only for Saturday, but also to allow Mother more leisure on Sunday and more time for washing on Monday.

A glance through the kitchen window — and that was as near as I dared usually go — revealed Mother and my eldest sister in long white overalls resembling two priestesses about to preside over secret rituals. At first their activities seemed almost leisurely: the dried-fruit-washing, apple-peeling, meat-mincing, and the rolling-out of pastry. Meanwhile the fire changed to a white glow and drew round the oven. Then quite suddenly the real action began as the two cooks set up a sort of production line which began at the end of the kitchen table nearest the door and finished at the opposite end near the oven. Patty pans were lined with prefabricated bits of pastry, fillings were slapped in, pastry covers dropped on. Scoops grabbed at the cake mix and shook out their contents on to flat baking tins. All these early items being small cooked quickly, and a regular flow in and out of the oven began. No ingredients were weighed, neither flour, fat nor fillings. Down the ten feet of table, rock cakes, mince tarts, meat pies, jam turnovers took shape. Into the oven they slid, pale and limp, only to emerge a few minutes later, brown and beautiful. With the fire drawing fast, cooking time was a matter for fine judgement; but Mother, like the village blacksmith, knew the vagaries of her ally.

Between the two women few words were needed; they were all dedication. The only pause was for Mother to remove steam or flour from her spectacles. After the small items came fruit pies in large enamel dishes, filled with apple, plum and damson. While all this was afoot, mounds of dough in large pancheons were 'rising' on the hearth, having been collected from the village baker after breakfast. So the final baking was of dough cakes crisped on the outside, moist and fruity within. I never thought the taste of bread lived up to the smell of the new-baked loaf. But the dough cakes Mother cooked encapsulated all the flavour that the nose had taught one to expect. Father agreed; he was sure there would be home cooking in heaven, and mass catering in the other place.

As twelve o'clock drew near, the heat and the action in the kitchen subsided. The cat dared to return to the hearth, and the Parson, with a fine sense of timing, looked in to say 'what a joy it was to see honest folk so fruitfully engaged', and to sample the fruits of Mother's labour, while he dried his gaitered feet before the kitchen fire.

Nowhere did the three elements of work, food and a warm bed come so close together as between the hours of seven and eight on a Saturday morning. Thankfully, my bedroom, shared with two brothers, was over the kitchen, and since the chimney stack passed by my bed, it was as good as central heating. Any time after seven o'clock the smell of frying bacon drifted in through the bedroom window. If Mother could not hear us moving, she banged on the ceiling with a brush and that warning was final. In our haste to be first at the washstand, it was not unusual to stub a toe on the chamber pot, or the hot brick we went to bed with. Occasional shouts up the stairs speeded us on. 'Wash behind your ears,' and 'Bring the candlestick down.' Nor dare we descend without emptying the 'slops' down the upstairs toilet. A beautiful warm fog of frying bacon always filled the kitchen, but as we entered, without even turning her head from the oven, Mother gave orders. 'Fill the coal buckets, feed the hens and shake the kitchen mats.' How did she know which one of us it was? There was no time for even 'Good morning'. Father said jokingly that farmers didn't talk much in case they wore their dentures out. Perhaps the wives were the same.

In a family of nine children, there is more example than precept. In my case, being third from the bottom, perfection always lay six steps ahead. My compensation was as mentor to the two below me. From the age of six we all did jobs. Weeding a cobbled yard with a broken knife, supervised by Mother from the kitchen window, was the first real work I remember. By the age of ten I realised that whether delousing the dog, carrying pig-swill, castrating the lambs or making hay, the whole family was like an embattled army, with Nature the main antagonist. The most we could do was win battles, never a whole campaign. Like the hobnailed boots drying out by the fire each night we went to bed preparing for the next assault. It was work without end, Amen.

In Mother's realm, the days of the week were of less significance than the work performed. Monday was wash-day, Tuesday market-day, Wednesday for bedrooms, Thursday downstairs rooms, Friday sewing and Saturday cooking. Bedroom day had special significance for me. The humblest village families, often those with many children, slept on mattresses stuffed with chaff or straw, obtained free from the farmers. Those a little more fur-tunate had 'flock' mattresses and pillows. But the Cramps and their peers 'lay warm' on down, and eiderdowns also topped every bed. So Wednesday was a day for really shaking and aerating the down; and mattresses received such a buffeting that not a ball of feathers remained. To go to bed on Wednesday night was sheer delight: I literally climbed up into bed and sank to sleep in a sea of feathers. Thurday's purge downstairs had more subtle impact: the aroma from furniture, new-shone with beeswax and linseed oil polish; the pungent smell of carbolic soap winning temporary victory over food bouquets in the kitchen; and the comforting yellow flames of the kitchen fire reflected in brass door knobs, the copper kettle and the warming pan.

WHETHER due to the right mixture of work, food, hygiene and sleep, or to my sturdy yeoman ancestors, my childhood was healthy. It was axiomatic in the family that you looked after what you had, and that included a Puritanic regard for fitness. We boys followed certain guide-lines laid down by Mother to combat bad weather. When doing a necessary outdoor task, it mattered not how wet you became. Feet might be sodden and rain running down your neck, but no harm would befall you if you kept working. If you didn't, 'You'd catch something you wouldn't easily get rid of.' So out in the fields in wet weather, fencing, muck knocking, spudding thistles or foddering, we ate our lunch sandwiches with scarcely a break. Consumption, the scourge of adolescents in my youth, was the disease Mother feared most. We were reminded of every local person who had died of 'chest trouble' in living memory — Mother's, that is. Though I never knew him, I had a vivid picture of how old Taylor ended: how he got so wet and cold sleeping in a ditch at lunchtime that he collapsed and died. When they found him his limbs were so stiff and distorted they buried him in a shroud because he would fit no coffin. I knew of every last moment of old Hackney who died of double pneumonia because he sold his jacket to pay for beer and insisted he could keep warm enough if he stuffed hay between his shirt and his skin. But most horrendous to my imagination was the fate of the schoolboy who went on a Sunday school 'treat' to Matlock, became hot through climbing and sat in a cave to cool off. 'Dead within a fortnight,' was Mother's verdict. Hence, when arriving home wet from the fields it was an article of faith to bath in the back kitchen and don dry clothes before eating a meal.

More specifically relevant to good teeth, we drank plenty of milk. Milk puddings or custard accompanied all other puddings, while bread and milk with added sugar was frequently our supper. But we also drank milk in less orthodox fashion. No one really knows the flavour of cows' milk who has not drunk it straight from the cow. It is an art only to be attempted by the accomplished milker, and quite on a par with drinking wine remotely from a Spanish flagon. The skill lies in turning the cow's teat sideways and upwards, and squirting the milk straight into the open mouth. The taste of the warm milk as it spatters off the back teeth or the hard palate is delicious, and as different from the bottled stuff as a fresh peach from a tinned one.

It is one thing to make good teeth, another to keep them. We cleaned our teeth with water and soap, and occasionally soot if we wanted to get an extra shine. Not until well into my teens did I encounter dentifrice. But I still maintain that my greatest aid to dental hygiene was the apple. Good 'eaters' were available all year round. Running the length of the house were attics in which were stored the apples from half an acre of orchard; cookers on one side, eaters on the other. Every night before getting into bed we groped our way up the unlit attic stairs, to select the variety of our fancy; 'groped' because candles were forbidden up there, and we relied on the pale light reflected from the bedroom. But dotted about the attic, and owing nothing to candlelight, were white plates from which came an eerie blue light — the phosphorescent glow of mouse bait. Despite cats, mice were always a pest in inaccessible places. Once they took a small denture of Mother's from a bedside stool, and vanished with it between the wide cracks that yawned between the floorboards where carpets did not reach.

Father had his own way with apples; he smothered them in the haystacks and only he knew where. He could go to a haystack, pull out a plug of hay, plunge his arm in up to the elbow and pull out scrumptious fruit, ripened in the hay's warmth. Perhaps the very hard water we drank from a well was also beneficial to teeth and bones. It was so rich in lime that the first touch of soap precipitated a white scum, while kettles became furred up in a month. No wonder we bought washing soda by the stone weight.

Spring Comes to Langton

BY THE TIME I was eleven, I was thought strong enough to undertake winter foddering of cattle and sheep with the help of a younger brother. We would set off into our clay world with a float drawn by Thimble the pony. Poor Thimble wore clay gaiters from November to March, and for twelve winters carried us from field to field, distributing fodder. Gateways were quagmires. The wet clay was as silky smooth as the mass on a potter's wheel. It sucked greedily at the feet and to navigate required a pumping action of the legs. The bullocks that awaited us in the gateways, appeared to have sawn-off legs as they stood knee-deep in mud, their foggy breath adding to the air of unreality. In every field, animals awaited us. We were their gods, but, like all gods, rationing the goodness. We were also their slaves. Having put bull to heifer and, as it were, created them, we must needs care for them also. Cutting hay from a stack was a devilish job. The hay-knife is like no other hand-tool on earth: crooked, heavy and operated by brute force. Today it decorates the walls of museums and old-world tearooms. Few can visualise the bent form of the labourer, fortified only by a breakfast of bread and dripping at 6.30 a.m., clinging to his narrow platform in the side of the haystack as he thrusts the knife into compacted hay. Yet my brother and I did this selfsame task, filled our cart and scattered the hay in the lee of hedges. It still carried the scent of a lost summer: clover, ryegrass, cowslips and 'totty' grass, and ox-eye daisies lay side by side in sweet-smelling death. The cattle, greedy as boys at a Sunday school treat, ran from heap to heap, sampling where they chose, and relishing the change from half dead grass, white over with hoar frost. How sad, I would think: the happier they are — good 'doers' we called them — the sooner they die. Only the fat die young!

Finches, sparrows, starlings and crows followed our course, feeding on hayseeds and whatever the torn earth yielded. We humans seemed the only foodless ones. Most gates had no hinges; only barbed wire kept them upright. If we complained to Father, he'd say hinges didn't earn anything. As we turned for home, Thimble trotted with real zest towards corn and a warm stable. We were not so different; we wanted the kitchen, meat, vegetables, and boiled apple pudding to follow.

When winter gave way to spring folks in our village could never agree about its timing except that it seemed to arrive somewhere between late February and mid-April. Most knew nothing of equinoxes, sunspot effects, or anti-cyclones moving up from the Azores. Each man preferred his own inbuilt personal barometer, whose mercury was the sights and sounds and smells of his daily life. If the sparrows were plundering the thatch on the roof and winter-sown broad beans were putting on growth, it could be spring. If the gardener noticed a surge of worms to the top soil, if you started to kick the clothes off the bed at night or chilblains suddenly vanished, then spring was surely just round the corner. Or she could announce herself with 'snow' on the blackthorn, greening on a sheltered garden hedge, browning on the aspen catkins, or reddening on the hens' combs. Were the bullocks more interested in the new spring 'bite' than in their hay? Was the rhubarb pushing through the muck put on it last autumn? Had anyone seen shrews hunting openly along hedgerow banks, or noticed primroses in bloom? Most certain sign of spring for some — could you feel the sun on your back and kick dust under your feet? Or if one day the aches of winter left your bones, you walked home to the singing of a skylark and gathered the first violet posy for the children, why should you not announce your spring?

'Gold is where you find it', and life is how you feel it.

In the presence of renewal, men tend to feel renewed, hopeful and forward-looking, and this was evident throughout our village. The poorest of folk took delight in putting 'lamb's tail' catkins or exploding white willow buds into a jar of water in their windows. Children wandering home from school found thrushes sitting so hard they could stroke their backs without causing them to leave the nest. At school, Nature lessons studied the habits of the blue periwinkle and violets, to say nothing of the miracles of the bursting peacock butterfly pupa or the evolution of frogspawn through tadpole to adult frog. Farm workers found snakes wriggling out of their warm winter quarters in manure heaps. Wise men now revealed how they had saved the seeds of onions, brussels, beans and peas from the previous year's crop, and subtle rivalries developed on the allotment patches. The postman began calling at houses never visited in a twelve month: some bold spirits, lured by adverts promising giant-sized vegetables, had written off for seed from distant Wales or Kent. Others made do with a visit to town on Saturday for packets of So and So's 'Satisfaction Seeds'. 'Don't believe in paying a lot for a fancy packet,' they would say. 'Besides, local grown seed suits the ground hereabouts.' With equal conviction they bought Scotch seed, ''cause taters like a change'. When mothers found themselves purging the house, when growing boys had boils on their neck, and fathers spent more time at the allotment than the pub, man's blood and spirit, like Nature's sap, was announcing spring.

In the Cramp household, the first whiff of spring in the form of mild south-westerlies was like a kick to a beehive; it sent the inhabitants into a frenzy of activity. There was a greater urgency about prompt rising of a morning and punctuality at meals. In any case, Mother's household spring cleaning acted as a lash to any who loitered around the house. She also proclaimed her need for young laying pullets to replace the old hens which were sold off as 'boilers'. One year Mother hatched and tried to rear her own chicks, but the brooder round which they nestled caught fire and burnt the lot, so she never tried again. At meal times there was much talk of rising milk yields with the first flush of grass, of lambs and how the numbers compared with last year, and of the need to 'shut fields up' so that the grass could grow on to become June hay. We young ones regarded this last announcement with horror. For us it meant boring week-ends 'stonepicking' to ensure none was left to damage mowing-machine blades. Bucket in hand we trudged up and down the grassy ridges with methodical precision, emptying each full bucket in the gateways to firm the ground for the carts. If at the end of the day there were only moderate amounts of stones to show, it was attributed to our dilatoriness, rather than our efficiency the previous year. Stone picking was followed by muck knocking before the field was finally rested.

In rotation, fields on the main farm were given a special dressing of manure. This came from the giant dunghill which accrued at home from cleaning out the cowsheds. So spring saw a procession of muck carts passing the length of the village to the Shangton farm and trailing their juices all the way. Villagers sniffed an appreciative nose at 'a bit of good stuff' and most days part of a load would be thrown off at somebody's front door to dress the garden. One man in a terrace house, who had no way to his back garden except by courtesy of his neighbours with whom he had quarrelled, wheeled his muck through his house.

A preliminary to Mother's spring cleaning was always the sweeping of chimneys, for soot built up from winter-long coal fires. But the much-used kitchen chimney sometimes anticipated Mother and fired furiously. I have memories of being awakened by a low sullen roar from the chimney stack near my bed, of the sound swelling like that from a deep throated organ. I would rush downstairs to perform my well-known drill. I can see Mother now, panic stricken by the suddenness, holding a frying pan full of bacon and burning soot; and my sister rolling back the hearthrug as the soot cascaded down. My job was to seize the sack used as a doormat outside the kitchen door, soak it at the pump, and drape it from the hood over the fire to control further soot falls. Then, with the door open, such a volume of air soon sucked up the chimney, that the soot went up instead of down. Outside, the chimney resembled an erupting volcano, but soon subsided. The sorry aftermath for me was 'bread-and-pull-it' for breakfast.

As the last dead leaves of winter are scoured from tree and hedge by the March winds; as the last seed pods rattle their emptiness on the bean trellis; as the gutters and ditches are cleansed of winter's dross by spring rains, man too feels the need to share in the cleansing process. The home, too much lived in through the winter days, has become prison-like. There is a need to open windows now and let in air and light; and to add colour in the home to vie with the burgeoning spring outside. The village resounds with dull thwacks as carpets are lifted, hung on clothes lines and beaten till all the dust (and some say the devil too) is beaten out of them. Up and down the village, washday now assumes monstrous proportions, as curtains, underblankets and mattress covers join the regular items. Nor is the need for 'a good blow' confined to Mondays. The really zealous women take weeks over their purge, giving as much care to reading the weather as the Romans did to examining entrails, as a guide to major enterprises. Patched and very worn articles are dried at night. Fine things are hung out by day, and left on view long after they are dry. The local shops run short of borax and soap, and even the rough women are civil to the local carrier, on whom they rely to fetch their goods from town.

But the clearest outward and visible sign, of the inward and spiritual grace which is reserved for the cleanly, is the steady trickle of people with buckets, moving to the bottom of the village to see Mr Busby. He will mix a distemper wash to any colour in the spectrum even as you watch. Not for him the whimsy of being confined to a newfangled colour-card.

'A little darker, Mrs Swingler? Too dark now? Just a touch more of green then. Slightly paler? A little yellow will do the trick.'

Personal satisfaction is guaranteed! As his estimates say, 'Everything to your complete satisfaction.' He will even hire you a distemper brush for a penny a day. Such is the liaison where producer and consumer live side by side, where a salesman must live next door to his faults; where bad material or workmanship become a matter for comment by the whole community, and the shame of it rests where it belongs.

Mrs Swingler, our washerwoman, normally comes only on a Monday. Now Mother hires her for a week. The menfolk in our house know that during that time life will be unbearable. From Mother, 'We must get the breakfast off the table otherwise Mrs Swingler will be here, kicking her heels and paid for doing it.' We've scarcely had our second cup of tea when Mother announces she doesn't want to see any of us till twelve thirty and then not for long. Dinners become poor emaciated things. Gone are the roasts, the chops, the fried gammon and time-consuming vegetables. Instead we have a surfeit of Irish stew and cold brisket with baked jacket potatoes. Puddings make way for bread and cheese, and eating apples from the attic.

The women are important as at no other time in the year and they know it! Virtue is on their side, and any inconvenience they inflict is twice blessed: it is necessary, and it lets the men know that running a house doesn't just mean 'flicking a feather duster'. Just occasionally we are hailed from the farmyard to move heavy furniture, but large and by we try to escape to the comparative predictability of pigs, cows and sheep. We are ordered (not asked) to keep cattle out of the orchard in case they bring the clothes lines down, and if we see storm clouds to announce the fact immediately.

Mrs Swingler's arms go redder as the days go by and her arm muscles bulge through much twisting of dolly pegs and turning of the mangle. Occasionally she appears in the orchard with a clothes basket on her hip, as washing appears and disappears. Even our man, who usually swears at Mrs Swingler because she's deaf, has a good word to say for her. In the house, ceilings are white-washed and walls colour-washed or repapered. Bedroom floors are scrubbed, windows repainted inside, and mouse-holes stopped up. The brass knobs on the bed ends shine like burnished gold. Wardrobes are turned out and re-papered inside with wallpaper remnants. We retire to bed in an aura of mothballs, carbolic soap and disinfectant.

Downstairs the purge is even more thorough. New coco-matting appears in the kitchen, the couch is re-covered in velvet, and Father's armchair has a new cushion and back-drape. New backing paper is placed behind the bacon flitches in the kitchen to prevent grease messing up the wallpaper. The carpenter planes the top of the kitchen table where twelve months of scrubbing has left hard grain and knots protruding. The oak beams in all rooms are restained a rich brown. Even the dog kennel is re-covered with felt and creosoted to kill the fleas.

By the end of March the deed is done. Visitors entering the house wrinkle an appreciative nose and say, 'My word you do smell clean.' The postman wonders if he dare knock on the newly varnished door and for a few days we are all slightly uneasy in our new surroundings. But we are proud really and want people to call. Mother is sweet-tempered again, and best of all, meals return to normal.

Of course Mother was mainly concerned with hygiene and clinical freshness. Only when Aunt Kate, Mother's teacher sister, arrived to spend Easter with us, were we reminded that daffodils looked attractive in the kitchen window, that the roses needed pruning, and that Nipper the terrier hadn't been bathed since Auntie was with us the previous year. In our family, certain jobs were never done until they screamed for attention, since they brought 'no grist to the mill'. When the bedroom windows wouldn't open or close because of the ivy, we cut the ivy. In haytime, wagonloads of hay were drawn home and went up the drive past the garden. Only when laurel hedge and bulging plum tree snatched at the loads, were the necessary amputations ruthlessly performed. When the shepherd dog grew flea-ridden, and scratched, and rattled his chain enough to disturb the family sleep he was put through the dip along with the sheep.

Father blessed the idea of 'summertime' and moved the clocks forward with the joy of a God moulding Nature to his desire. He was sure the idea came from the Tories and would quote, 'Vote Red and lie in bed'. He was also sure that man was made for work. It was a livelihood and a way of life, a medicine and a therapy, an antidote to crime and a religion.

Unwillingly to School

AT FIVE YEARS OLD I went to school as willingly as a pig to market; made a good deal of noise on the way but kept quiet once penned on arrival, acknowledging 'force majeure'. It made no difference that I was not alone, for I never remember a time when at least two Cramps did not make the journey. Sometimes we kicked a ball the whole way, or in dry weather the cap of some mawkish boy would briefly be substituted. Stone throwing amused older boys. A ready-made armoury lay underfoot in the metalled road and the stone heaps dotted about for repair. The telegraph posts were targets and sometimes the white insulators. One hard winter when crows were too weak to outrange us, we killed several. One poor lad took them home saying his dad loved crow pie. In spring home-coming was birds'-nesting time and most labouring families ate the eggs of blackbird, thrush, woodpigeon and moorhen. When my brothers gathered the latter, they always marked the first three with a pencil and left them for 'sitting'. All subsequent ones were taken. Hungrier families were not so discriminating. High summer of course was blackberry time and we ate our way to school and back. Homeward bound we washed away stains in a cattle trough on the village outskirts, to avoid Mother's wrath.

In my early school days girls always seemed older and wiser and more self-assured, carrying a comfortable air of home around with them and treating school as a necessary but very subordinate activity. One girl claimed mystical powers. When we boys pressed our ears to telegraph poles we heard nothing save singing wires. Alice claimed to hear voices. She was never at a loss to entertain us with lovers' conversations, sons speaking to dying mothers, or rich ladies ordering fur coats for themselves and dolls' houses six feet high for their children. Her delivery was so dramatic we often believed her.

One half-witted boy provided us with constant amusement. He frequently ate his lunch, bread plus an onion, on the way to school. Just as often he went home at lunchtime, thinking it was end of day. He never learned to write but compensated by keeping the Headmaster's garden weeded. He possessed neither vests nor pants but once briefly sported a rabbit skin waistcoat. Jimmy could throw and climb like the rest of us and seemed not to register pain. His father, a drover, had vanished years ago and Jimmy helped his mother with a smallholding. His sojourn in the village ended sadly when his mother could no longer cope. Three men in a black ambulance fetched him away. They trapped him in the cowshed manger, where he often slept on his back in the afternoon, and sedated him. His only legacy was a pile of comics, which his mother secretly bought him, though he was man-grown.

Our school, endowed by the Rev. William Hanbury, had near-cathedral proportions. A few obstinate sparrows roosted on the roof trusses of lofty classrooms and occasionally anointed our desks. We were ruled by the magic of three — a triumvirate of staff. Each member occupied one of three large rooms containing three classes. This nine-step education ladder served to sieve and sharpen the wits of children from six villages. Few who entered the Hanbury Charity Foundation School at age five failed to emerge with some degree of literacy at fourteen. What repetition failed to inculcate, the cane did.

My infant school education was uninspired but thorough. We wrote on slates with slate pencils that whistled as we scraped our words. A daub of spit served to make corrections and insertions as efficiently as a word processor. Coloured chalk on grey paper was the basis of our art. In plasticine, of course, I modelled farm animals.

The magic of poetry was used to gild some subjects. 'One, two, buckle my shoe. Three, four, knock at the door' made even the dullards seem numerate. And most poems were heavy with moral precept.

To make the watering habits of sixty mixed infants coincide was beyond even the powers of Mrs Dickinson. So we 'Please Miss-ed' when hard pressed and she was adept at divining genuine need. The occasional mistake was soon rectified with the aid of a Tortoise Stove in winter. In summer, authority provided a pair of spare pants which fitted boys and girls indifferently. When I left the Infants Department at seven I was well versed in the three Rs and knitting! But my most abiding memories are the wall pictures: Moses lugging the Ten Commandments down Sinai amidst thunder and lightning without getting wet, and the unforgettable Abraham offering Isaac – the father with knife poised over his prostrate son, but his eye falling on a ram in a thicket. The whole business appalled me — not least the waste of a good ram. My God preferred live animals that grew fat and were sold at profit.

The Middle School was controlled by an irascible spinster. She lived with her aged mother in a house linked by a corridor to our classroom. She frequently slipped out for domestic reasons, usually after caning one or other of us to ensure order meanwhile. The nearer to lunch the more frequent the journeys till the maddening smell of cooking drove us to sample our own snacks and risk the penalties. Miss Banner had a wry neck and hunched shoulders. Some boys said it was caused by caning over a lifetime. She caned and bruised our hands and then caned us again because we wrote badly. We learned much through fear and little from joy, even in singing. For three years we sang from a Tonic Sol Fa chart draped over a blackboard. The pointer indicating the notes was the same one used to cane us; it moved menacingly up and down the scales. I was glad to escape to the Upper School. The Headmaster was a stern man but the wart on his nose, the twinkle in his eye and a rotund belly seemed to say that he understood life's imperfections and sometimes even enjoyed them. He punished and praised; scolded and laughed. He abhorred timetables and pursued where our interests led, though rather too often they led to his private garden where those not wanting to learn did digging. So the class divided and in his garden we measured rods, poles and perches, and the circumference of his apple trees and the weight of his crops. We studied earthworms and spiders, birds and bees. We recited poetry in summer shade — while others dug, sowed or reaped. And only once did a boy jib at his chosen labour: when he realised that the manure came directly from the school earth toilets. But an apple or two, which the Head usually carried, settled the matter instantly.

Though the school timetable said PE, we did none, unless to stand on our desks and beat our arms to keep warm in wintertime. Nor did we have Games. Yet once a year at summer term end, the School Charity endowments decreed Sports Day. Then we sprinted, three-legged it, jumped and gyrated as if this had been our daily diet. For a grand finale the Governors hurled handfuls of coins into the air. I remember deciding that whereas everyone else leaped up to grasp the manna I could fare better by crouching and gathering my spoils from the grass. And I did!

Our village had always one or two wild boys: social unfortunates, delighting in devilry. But to us they seemed as natural as boils on the bottom in springtime, painful but necessary, part of our young generation, an inevitable social eruption. School was their prison, village life their therapy. Most grew to viable manhood, and I never knew one go to gaol.

'Tiger' Jimmy was one such lad. Origin unknown, name uncertain; he lived with a person he variously called aunt and grannie. Mostly his clothes were tattered and his shoes leaky; or if they were not he took care to make them so, for he delighted in adversity. We gave him the attention he craved and he played to our fearful gallery. Sometimes he turned up at school in fine new clothes, probably from an orphanage or benefactor. But Tiger had a way with these. He would rip off jacket buttons to show his strength, and swallow one if he had a good audience. He cut the tongues from his shoes to make catapult slings. He never had a handkerchief, and wiped his nose on his sleeve till it shone white. Most front teeth were missing; the survivors were blackened and chipped. Where hair should be was an outcrop of bristles, each growing from a grime-black spot. A water mark round angle of jaw and chin showed the limits of Tiger's washing, so that viewed from the side he appeared to be wearing a mask. He wore scabs on his knees like armour plate, and in summer drank water from puddles in the road.

He was caned every day at school because he wanted to be. A daily dose of our adulation was better to him than food and drink. So to earn the cane he would fall off his seat, put ink on his eyelids, conjure up foul smells from nowhere, tie girls' plaits together if he sat behind them, and devise a score of sly tricks. On winter nights he had revenge on the Headmaster, tied cotton to his door knocker and pulled it from a distance, and spread muck in his porch so he walked straight in it.

Not a bad boy really; just a boy of his times.

Thanks to the generosity of the Rev. Hanbury, our Governors controlled rich endowments. With all the zeal shown when spending the money of others, annually on prize day they improved our young lives with books and food. Prize day was a lucky dip, for winners were not informed beforehand. Everybody was in with a chance. The Head sought for and found virtue to reward in the most unlikely places. There were prizes for good attendance, good conduct, good effort; for neatness, diligence, courtesy, helpfulness. We rewarded knitting and gardening, spelling and singing, reading and writing, essays and sums. Further, we found so many subtle degrees of excellence, extending so far down the scale, that there was little reject stuff left over for the Devil to stir up envy. There were first, second, third and fourth prizes for certain; and several more if charity investments had yielded well. The effect was magnetic. As prize day approached, hooligans grew tame; slackers waded through spring floods to avoid absence; 'duffers' who used more spit than pencil on their slates grew lettuces big as cabbages on their school plots. Girls who had stumbled over 'knit one, purl one' knitted acres of scarf – with a little help from mother. Not a parent, not a child, had anything to say against prize day. Every family in five parishes could boast a winner, if not this year, last — or it could be next, for every leaver received a prize for having stayed the course.

In honour of prize day, children were decked out in their Sunday best. Mothers took no chances. 'It's the end a' May, an' I were goin' ter buy our gal a summer frock anyway. Besides, yer never know yer luck do yer? And the kids like to dress up for the treat a'terwards.'

My first prize day came as a shock. Everyone seemed to have been forewarned except me. So I was puzzled that May morning why everyone looked so smart. The girls in particular were 'dolled up to the nines', with new 'pinners', stockings, hair ribbons and frocks. I saw with incomprehension one older girl display new knickers to her friends. But only when I heard her talking of 'prizes' and 'Treats' and 'our mum comin' to collect us a'ter the do', did the truth dawn. A moment of panic and the wobbly belly feeling that surprise often gave me. Would the school governors inspect our underwear? An older boy reassured me. I took further comfort when I saw a girl that rumour said possessed no knickers. She wore instead long vests fastened between her legs with a safety pin. If she was safe, I was. Only now, and for the second time in as many minutes, another great truth dawned on me. The reason I was wearing my best jacket wasn't simply because a button was missing from my usual one. And I was wearing the shoes with hooks over the eyes, not because my others were still damp. Mother had manoeuvred me into best clothes under false pretences, in case ... in case the unthinkable happened, and I won a prize. In new clothes I was always as unhappy as a hen in full moult. I must abjure puddles, wrestling on the roadside and climbing fences. I must return home at the end of the day like a prize animal and undergo inspection.

In our family, parading new clothes was taboo. 'To put a fortune on your back' was a quick way to ruination. Only wastrels dressed in la-di-da clothes. When we wore new items, we constantly apologised for putting aside 'good old ones'. Muddled by this philosophy, but wearing new clothes, I made the best of my case, rubbed the brass buttons on my jacket and marvelled at the smoothness of my rump in the absence of patches. And after all, I had been spared the horror of wearing a blouse like 'Bertie the darling', a boy in my own class. His voluminous clothes were chosen to hide his scraggy frame. In his first term at school his mother visited him every lunchtime, for he was only four and a half. She came where the boundary rails of the playground were screened by bushes, pressed her breast between the bars and suckled him quickly. He died young just the same.

The morning at school was pleasantly different. Seating the whole school in the big room was like a military operation. All must be familiar with the maze whose exit lay next to the Governors' seats, and the prizes. Being an infant on a front row bench I was spared that however, though at lunchtime the likes of me were subjected to ordeal by water. The Headmaster's wife confronted us with a bucket of tepid water, soap, clean rags and a

common towel. When flesh on face and knees was sufficiently revealed we were ordered to the toilets 'Whether
you want to or not.' Most of us wanted, and made so
much of this unusual ceremonial that Mrs Dickinson
squawked at us over the top of the toilet wall and threatened us with lock out from prizes and food.

Promptly at two o'clock, the Headmaster, whiskers
new-trimmed and a gold hunter watch chain riding on his
belly, led the Governors in. 'Be seated, children,' he said in
a warm and honeyed voice, that left some of us still
standing, for normally he just barked, 'Sit.' Closely
opposite me sat the Vicar, yellow skin, weasel-thin voice
and dandruff all over his black cassock. He called on God
to 'plenteously reward us' for our labour. I dwelt on the
profit and loss aspects of this statement, as I sat with
bowed head. I watched an ant crawl over his gaiters,
glanced up at the 'dewdrop' he wore like a pearl on the
end of his nose, and was startled into life by his loud
'A-men'.

Then up on our feet to sing about 'Trelawny' and twenty
thousand Cornishmen wanting 'to know the reason why'.
I never did know the answer, or where the river Tamar
was, but I entered into the spirit of things. The wild
swishing wand of Miss Banner, Head of Middle School,
conducted us. Her baton swung dangerously close to my
face and I fancied I felt the draught. To avoid going
cross-eyed, I looked beyond it and watched her colour
rise. At the end of verse one, the top of her bosom —
never in view till this day — grew pink. Verse two and the
colour had mounted to her neck. As Trelawny's men
marched on, she was red to the roots of her hair and
mouthing horribly to keep us in time and tune. The end
came with a downward chop of the baton, so sudden that
I was happy to have escaped injury. The Vicar whinnied
our praises and the Head smiled enough to reveal the top
of his dentures, so I knew we had done well.

As prizegiving proceeded my bottom grew strangely

numb. I missed the thick worsted patches on my back-side. But I followed orders: arms folded, right over left, pink knees together and feet tucked under the bench, one behind the other. As the Head announced the awards, the Lord of the Manor presented the prizes, every one leather bound. 'Bully' Barber, looking mild as milk, was rewarded for prowess at games, though 'dirty tricks' would have been a better description. 'Weedy' Perkins, a midget of a boy, but fourteen years old, received a leaver's prize. He died before he could read it, and it was buried with him. 'Lil' Wood, one of nine children, was honoured for sewing a patchwork quilt. And so the parade went on: no one was lost in the desk maze, no ink was spilled on the floor, no trace of talent was ignored; not, that is, until the name of 'Bogey' Barton was announced. (They called out 'James' of course.) Only I and two others guarded a horrible secret. Lunchtime excitement had proved too much for Bogey; he had messed his trousers and fled home a mile away, but not before swearing he would be back for the treat at four o'clock. Twice his name was called — then on to the next, with never a thought for Bogey, who, finding his house locked up had to wash down in a cattle trough and hide his loins in a haystack till his mother returned.

The Headmaster and the Lord of the Manor droned on. The spontaneous clapping became a perfunctory duty. It withered like the sound from crow-scaring clappers in tired hands and soon contained as much warning as welcome. Concentration flagged, heads lolled, bellies rumbled; this despite the ultimatums flung by the eyes of Miss Banner as they ploughed up and down the desks. The Vicar's chin dropped to his chest in sleep or silent prayer. The room grew hot with the scalding tension of three hundred bodies. Now and again, harsh smells drifted headhigh before climbing to the raftered ceiling.

Suddenly my mind found a focus to combat sleep. The diminishing piles of prizes became balanced by the in-

creasing prospect of food. I calculated that those trestle
tables now empty of books could accommodate a thousand
mince pies and ten thousand sausage rolls. Another pile
of books gone. Room now for an ice-cream tub big as a
milk churn. Why did tubs have to be small and double-
lined to take up valuable space? 'Joe, John, Mary, Bert.'
Who were these people? Simply a prelude to the main
business, the treat to end all treats. 'Scatty' Bromley,
though he could not always be relied on, had said his
mother was helping serve tea this year, and not even our
biggest farm wagon would carry the food we had to eat
between four o'clock and sundown. I mused on the possibility of holding a cream horn in one hand, a banana
stripped to the waist in the other, and taking alternate
bites. But on no account must I forget the jelly business.
Most kids asked for red, so you got more if you opted for
green — and the taste was the same! Oh yes. Keep off the
potted meat made by Butcher Berry: little better than
gristle and floor sweepings, Mother said. Ham was a
better bet. Hope they don't put mustard on it. A pickled
onion would go well. But that would occupy the left hand,
which should be grasping the 'afters'. Hunger slowly
devoured me; belly betrayed eyes, eyes betrayed ears.
From my seat the Headmaster was obscured by the Parson,
now drooped like a living question mark. But the Headmaster's hand was visible still. Attached to a mechanical
arm, it plunged out, grasped a book, lifted, vanished; then
returned and did it again and again. Ladders of sunlight
slanted through the high windows, and the books danced
in a mirage of dust, only to reappear as giant slices of
currant loaf. The owner of the hand grabbed piece after
piece. Suddenly the hand addressed me with a doomsday
voice like the one that bothered my dreams: 'Harold
Cramp: first prize for Infants Class Two.' My brain was
caught between currant loaf and a mountain of trifle
surrounded by snow made of whipped cream, but my
body responded. I tried to rise, but could not. Every time

my bottom left the seat it returned just as quickly. The metal hooks of my shoes were firmly locked into one another: I was helpless as a horse in hobbles.

It was now that I enrolled Miss Banner in my private hall of fame. With a speed that did her credit, for she had a wry neck, she bent down and released me. Four quick paces and a handshake later, I grasped *The Princess and Curdie* and, crimson faced, scuttled to my bench; book on lap, back straight, feet underneath — and securely locked again. My prayer, that I should not win another prize that day, was answered. I 'God-save-the-Kinged' with bowed legs, glared at the Parson's waistcoat and stood on my ankles. Then suddenly the crisis passed; the Governors made their exit. I was free to unshackle and gaze at my prize. 'Presented by the Governors of the Hanbury Trust to . . .' was engraved in letters of gold. At that moment, I thought I was worth no less.

After the prizegiving, an airing to crisp our appetites while tea was laid on trestle tables. Junior toilets were separate from seniors', but the pressure to arrive there was still great. Most of us had no trouser 'flies'; they were sewn up against weather and accident. So we raised one trouser leg as we ran, and by the time we rounded the toilet screen wall, we were committed to action. The floor was awash, but nobody cared, so back to the entrance porch at speed, paddling a damp track across the asphalt yard. Two boys hadn't even left the door, fearing the signal for tea would find them in the toilets with a handicap of thirty yards. Finally they compromised and used the coke bunker nearby.

The school door opened. Miss Banner frowned, sniffed the air ominously and led us in. Class Two Infants were at the far end, so we marched through valleys of food to arrive at our promised land. Mountains of scones, buns and rock cakes stood high as my head. Multicoloured jellies (I had been cheated again) dithered at their base. Placed zig-zag fashion down every table were pyramids of sandwiches. Though still shuffling along I divined salmon, ham, tomato, fishpaste and the inevitable potted meat. We were nearly there now. Always avoid the end seat; I learned that at home. Best have food to right and left. I hung back a little and finished up halfway down the table opposite a pile of cherry slice and next to a frail-looking girl who seemed unlikely to offer much competition. So far so good. More instructions. 'Start with sandwiches everybody. Tea will be brought to you; now grace. For what we are about to receive, . . .' Whoever seated us forgot one thing: we were infants and the trestles were too high. We took off our jackets and sat on them; now we had more leverage. A chumbling silence fell on the room, like the murmur from a contented beehive.

After the first fierce rapture we became more choosy, ate the heart out of sandwiches and clamoured for tea to wash down reluctant crusts, or slipped them under the table. Then, suddenly, like a battle call, 'Start on the cakes.' Deep-throated silence again, as we got our second wind. Skyscrapers of Easter plumcake were reduced to their foundations. Ranging hands plundered the cherry heaven before my very eyes. A moment of anxiety when the word 'shortage' spluttered through a cloud of crumbs from a boy to my right. False alarm though: he was merely calling for 'shortcake', but it proved so crumbly he chewed himself to a standstill.

Another quarter of an hour gone, and we were faltering again. Rock cakes were avoided, sponge cake was at a premium. Some slight complaining, till like battle weary soldiers, we launched the final attack. 'Operation Jelly' began. To avoid casualties, helpers served us; neat trembling sections for the first helping, a crumbling iceberg mass for the second. Through gaps in our teeth, we forced jelly into our cheek spaces, like marmosets; and still we swallowed. A final topping-up followed as we filed past the ice-cream and bore our cornets back like victory torches after a marathon.

'For what we have received, may the Lord . . .' Exit past the ruins of a beautiful memory. At the door we received an apple and an orange, in case our homeward walk revealed that in some remote corner of our tiny frames a bubble of hunger still lurked. As we lolloped onto the highway, Bogey came round the corner at a gallop, paused, realised the awful truth of things, and went roaring home.

When I reached home I was quite surprised to find that tea wasn't laid.

Saturday, Sunday,
Washday, Market Day

I WAS WAKENED by itching toes; my chilblains were driving me mad. Bad circulation, mother said, though I didn't believe it. Five miles daily to school and week-end work on the farm saw to that. Though only fourteen, the hummocks of muscle on my shoulders were almost a disfigurement.

But back to my toes. The previous night I had dabbed them with piddle from the pot under my bed, an infallible cure the village folk said. No good to me though. 'Try brushing them!' This from Cecil who was simmering to life in the bed beside mine. I did as he said, with a clothes brush, and the result was sheer delight; almost worth having the chilblains. For a few moments, I slid back into my feather heaven. Bubbles of warmth flowed round me as the duck-down oozed round my legs, caressed my shoulders, nuzzled my arms. I was not so awake that the Saturday world intruded; not so asleep I couldn't enjoy my floating cloud of comfort. Now and again in the gathering light, wallpaper roses peeped through my eyelids, insisting on being counted. But determined still to resist the day, I poked at the crystals of 'sleep' that always gummed up my morning eyes, screwed my face in the pillow and tried to resurrect sleep. I saw only roses, spray bleeding into red spray; small buds and fullblown flowers in unending columns, uncountable now, as they swayed in an unfelt wind, till they clogged my brain and I finally slept again.

'Are you moving?' A chastening voice from the kitchen below, followed by an echoing broadside, as Mother struck the great oak beam with a poker to jerk the sleep from our eyes. Cecil leaned out of bed and smote the floor with his hand to give a semblance of action. 'Idle as a foal,' Mother called him. Really he was growing fast and needing plenty of sleep. I lunged across the room to the washstand, propelled by the gradient of the old oak floor, so steep and uneven in parts that even a half-filled chamber pot could sometimes threaten spillage. The marble-topped washstand challenged my courage. Water and flannel were stone cold and I yelped with the shock. Cecil took the hint, spilled out of bed and dry towelled the blood to his cheeks. Then he splashed water freely on his hair to part it, and in the finish, looked like a swimmer new-come from the pool, though no water had touched his face.

Our staircase was twisting and unlit, like a piece chopped out of a castle turret. Grasping the banister and keeping a toehold we emerged by touch into the sitting room, cool, quiet and uncluttered, the neutral zone between night and day. Five short paces more and the kitchen assaulted us, battered us with orders, drowned us in heat, then rescued us with the promise of food. From her operations centre in front of the great range fire, Mother, aided by my sister Muriel, manoeuvred nine of us through a breakfast of porridge, bacon and toast in thirty minutes. Orders, action and comment from Mother precluded all conversation. Only Mother knew the secret of each next move; only she could prevent chaos. One break in her thought pattern, and it seemed to me that the cauldron of porridge would erupt over the hearth, the milk boil over, the toast burn, the bacon frizzle to a cinder, and cups of tea never survive their journey down the length of the kitchen table. Listen, obey, keep your head down and eat, was the safest policy, indeed the only one. Mother's voice shuttled about the kitchen. 'Watch the milk; save a little for the late lambs. Careful with the kettle Father; handle's all sooted up. Don't clatter your porridge spoons boys, you weren't dragged up in a ditch.

Dick is in a mess; scrape the porridge off his jersey. Stir that cat off the hearth, or somebody's going to get scalded. Pull the blower out, Muriel, and draw the fire, there's dinner to be thought of. Put a bit more coal on but leave some glee for toast. And don't scatter dust unless you want to Zebo the grate all over again. Here comes the postman; time I had a letter from Aunt Kate. Steady with that kitchen door; don't want a pother of smoke. Eat more bread with your bacon boys; fill you out a bit. More tea Father? There's just a dram in the pot. Harold, eat Cecil's fried bread. What's the matter with him? Left his bacon rinds too. Looks bilious; yellow as a guinea. Epsom salt for him tomorrow. Finished Harold? Then leave the table and start on the hens. When you've cleaned them out kill the young cockerel and then. . . .'

Orders followed me as I moved to the door. Cecil squeezed after me to the lifting mists of a fine spring morning and the freedom of the farmyard.

We went straight to the large henhouse with barrow and shovel to purge the droppings. Five red leghorn hens on nestboxes stirred not an inch. Some clucked broodily, so I decided to investigate and plunged a hand under each in turn; nothing except the hot stickiness of damp feathers and protesting squawks at this invasion of female privacy. The young cockerel seemed to sense impending doom and stabbed his neck blindly through the wire mesh fence. I hated my job really. It seemed obscene to destroy the beauty of the blood-red comb, the scarlet wattles and the neck where feathers of red and gold arch over in ever-changing rainbows. But I consoled myself — my Biology teacher was right. God created a system where life preys on life in an endless chain of destruction. So who was I to outsay God? Besides, Mother's orders were more immediate than God's. I grabbed the cockerel's legs in my left hand; he hung upside down, and quite submissive. My right hand gripped his neck close behind the head. A quick pull down and the neck was broken. Wings flapped briefly. I looked up. The hens pecked as usual. Cecil was being sick. Biliousness . . .? His turn to kill would soon come.

For a few minutes we watched Father and older brothers de-horning calves: a bloody business, the crushing of horn buds, and accompanied by much bawling. The job was just done when a new neighbour looked over the boundary hedge; a textile man from Leicester who had bought the house of a gentleman farmer recently deceased. In a peevish voice he complained of farmyard noises, from the cows, calves and dogs, from the rolling of milkchurns and even the cockerel's morning salutations. Further, the smell of manure disgusted his visitors.

Father answered quietly, and those of us listening had a lesson in teaching lessons.

'Do I understand you are a vegetarian?'

'Certainly not. What gave you that idea?'

'Then you eat beef and drink milk. Bullocks and cows start as little calves, and they, like all babies, will protest now and again. And be thankful for manure: you'll need a lot for your garden.'

'Well, there's reason in everything,' came the querulous reply, though I knew that Father's quiet answer had taken him off guard.

Father continued, 'Whenever you feel like reasoning with a bawling bull, come round. As for the cockerels, this one won't bother you any more.' Here he seized the cockerel from me and held it aloft and continued, 'And now we have work to do. I'm thinking of building some calf pens here.' I knew he wasn't, but I liked his answer. I'd never seen Father like this before. Normally a man of few words, he could display startling eloquence when he scented some challenge to his way of life, especially from someone with no roots in the soil.

I suddenly remembered I must fetch the Saturday dough from the village bakery; one of the breakfast-time orders. I never lingered outside the bakehouse door.

Dough's funny stuff, must be kept warm, so I plunged straight in. Wonderful how one small wooden door can keep two worlds apart. Outside, the moist May air touched with ten o'clock sunshine, and fragrant as a dog-rose. Inside the door, heat forbids breath; air must be tasted: a hot compound of yeast, wheaten flour and crusty bread. The bakehouse was never so white and still as today, as if a flour storm had raged, then calmed, and left in its wake a flour desert. My feet made noiseless Man-Friday prints on a powdered floor. The sun shone whitely in, to show age-blackened beams adorned with white lace cob-webs, where long legged spiders strode over flour-drifts. And there stood the baker, dressed in flour, blinking through white-burdened lashes, but speaking no word. Then this dough-man shook himself, briefly vanished in his own white cloud, and emerged as Mr Freestone, the real life baker. 'Just shouldering a sack of flour from the loft when it burst,' said he. 'Expect you've come for the dough.' I ran hotfoot with the story and the dough to find Mother waiting for me, irritably aproned for the Saturday cook. I felt quite cheated that she was more concerned with the state of the dough than the fate of a baker drowned in flour.

One more Saturday job: off to Kibworth for the meat, with Cecil for company. Two things concerned us: first, a sealed note to the butcher — most unusual; secondly, two pence left over from the sale of a rabbit we had caught. At journey's end both matters were soon resolved. As the butcher read the note his colour rose from red to puce to purple. 'Your Mother don't want no fat and no bone but fifteen pounds of solid lean. Where the devil does that grow on a bullock?' He whetted his knife with a fury that drove Cecil behind me, and mooched round his hanging carcasses stopping now and then to glare at me as if I were the cause of his problem. But knife and saw soon went to work and we left the shop with the joint in a large straw bag suspended from a pole which rested on our shoulders as we walked in tandem. Rag-a-muffin boys dodged under our moving bridge, as we made for the shops. Cecil was taken with a pile of chewing gum, labelled on top at a penny. When given a tiny packet of four, he soon changed his mind and bought a yard of Spanish juice, a liquorice that looked like a bootlace. I settled for four mint humbugs, flavoursome and, above all, lasting, if one could resist the crunching stage and carry the last delectable marble in a hollow cheek.

We grumbled our way home with the meat, which grew heavier as the sun rose higher. When we had nothing except black lips to show for the liquorice and only the mint on our breath to remind of the humbug delights, we turned to nibbling sourgrass and tender hawthorn shoots. Suddenly, Nature in the raw came to rescue us from boredom. As we sat resting on a five-barred gate, watching the sky larks lift on currents of warming air, two small creatures headed towards us across the open field. Or was it one, trailing a shadow that was far too thin to be real? Soon we discerned the puppet form of a young rabbit, propelled by agonised jerks of fear; and slithering in its wake through the tufted spring grass, a weasel, whiplash thin. The *dénouement* we witnessed had begun elsewhere. The weasel must not close on the rabbit too soon. First the increasing prospect of death must be allowed to wreak its paralysis; time is of the essence. Only when terror has crippled the victim can the final blow be struck. With back arched high and hind-quarters tucked tightly under belly, constricted muscles allowed only feeble scrapings at the turf, each accompanied by a death scream. Ears lay flat along the head, as the creature tried to shrink back into a tight womb of nothingness. But the eyes would not obey and grew to black pools into which flowed the final distillations of fear. Almost at our feet, the weasel sprang at the rabbit's throat and the two flung over in a tangled mass.

Thus far, Cecil and I, tableau figures on a gate, had

spoken no word, but now we sprang from the gate as one, and beat at the weasel with our feet. Taken by surprise it fled back into the field and we gave chase with the carrying pole. Halfway across the field we caught up, and spent our anger in a few killing blows. Then we marvelled that so slight a creature, now quite beautiful in death, should daily do murder to survive. When we returned to the gate, the rabbit had vanished. 'Perhaps,' said Cecil, with unconscious irony, 'we'll catch him one day when hunting with Nipper.' We picked up the meat basket and shook out the invading ants. In the field, carrion crows were gathering near the weasel carcass. Overhead, the larks sang on. Surely, I thought, they must never look down.

Our journey ended in comparative comfort, for down the road came a pony-drawn tub. As it drew close it zig-zagged erratically, stopping well short of us. The outfit, I knew, belonged to John Forman, a drunken gentleman farmer. But he was missing and the tub door was open. Thinking he might have fallen out, we climbed in and drove back the way we had come. Round the first bend, a swaying figure waved in the middle of the road. He was too far gone to recall our names, save that we were 'Hector's lads'. We guessed what had happened when twice more on the journey home our friend disembarked to make water.

Mother was pleased with the Sunday joint. When we outlined the morning's events, she said we should have caught the rabbit, and not bothered with a useless weasel.

Saturday afternoon was school homework time, so up to my bedroom for encounters with Algebra, Latin and English, the latter an essay on 'Pleasures of the Imagination'. I toyed with the idea of imagining that humans lived in a world inhabited by giant weasels that each day hounded a man to death while everyone else went quietly about his business. But fearing the reception such alarming thoughts would encounter at school, I wrote instead about daydreams. Just when I'd finished, Cecil appeared, recalling our plan to go bird's-nesting, but lamenting that he still had a poem to write for homework and no idea how to start. To save time I scribbled three verses. 'Death of a rabbit' wasn't much of a poem but at least it put my musing to some use.

Bird's-nesting meant wandering, following hedgerows, plunging into ditches, exploring ponds, and watching for telltale signs: the flight of a startled bird, or the shadow patch high in the hawthorn hedge that indicated the nest of pigeon or magpie. Jackets worn inside out in case of damage, we looked like walking scarecrows. We 'blew' our eggs on the spot, using a thorn to prick holes at either end. The empty shells we carried under our hats. Eggs like the moorhens', of course, we preserved for eating. These came mainly from nests floating on beds of reeds or riding at anchor on branches, dangling over ponds. With a bent spoon attached to an elder stick, we eased out our prizes one by one; Sunday breakfast, we knew, would be a feast.

Two miles from home with a bleeding hand, a thorn in my knee and a pigeon's nest just out of reach, I suddenly had a vision of a Saturday dough cake tea. Straightaway, the towline of hunger, one end anchored to the kitchen table, drew us back by the shortest route. We trotted purposefully, only pausing to adjust the eggs in our hats. When a distant clock struck five there was panic, for that was the deadline for tea. Five minutes later we approached the kitchen with a plan to dilute Mother's anger. We would enter with the ten moorhens' eggs in my hat and say, 'We've brought tomorrow's breakfast.'

To our amazement we were greeted with smiles all round. Tea had not yet begun, the dough cakes were intact and there was honey as well as jam for tea. There was also much talk of 'Uncle Foster', of whom I had never heard. 'Fancy him popping off so smartly. And who would have thought the old boy had money tucked away. Lucky

The Organisers of the village fête: Sergeant Barker is in the back row with Mr Freestone the baker in a bowler hat and Zack Busby the carpenter next to him. Brother Bob is second from right in the front row.

Church Langton Rectory, which successfully insulated the Vicar from most of his parishioners

The church at Shangton, 'a sad little hamlet that died with the field enclosures'

Grandpa Cramp from Shangton in his pony tub

the housekeeper didn't get her hands on it.' Gradually, I learned the truth of things. By the four o'clock afternoon post Mother had learned that she had inherited several hundred pounds, and it seemed my life was transformed. Blood on my hands and no reprimand from sister Muriel; four dough cakes at a sitting, instead of the usual two; a lace-edged tablecloth usually reserved for Sunday; and no one urging us on through tea, to get milking done, to get an early night, to start Sunday work early, to . . .

My vision of sweetness and plenty, cakes and honey every day, even perhaps for breakfast, was suddenly dashed. Father had quickly consumed the legacy in bullocks and two new fields he hoped to buy; Mother talked of a long holiday, and a new wing on the house. Brother Stanley urged a new car. As my dough-cake world receded, I tucked into the honey before that too departed. I never did know what happened to all that money. I do know we never again had four dough cakes for tea.

As a child I never did come to terms with Sunday. It was no sort of a day, dedicated to nothing, with little zeal shown for work, play or church. Mother's Puritan conscience, product of a strict childhood, hung over us like a pall. 'Get your jobs done, so that you can change into your best clothes; it's Sunday.' Or, 'Take this note to the washerwoman, but comb your hair first and don't forget it's Sunday. And don't play in the street, folks might be resting.'

Mother seldom went to church: 'Somebody's got to cook the dinner!' But occasionally she would say, 'Time one or another of us put in an appearance at church.' This was the signal for Cecil and me to be bundled up-stairs to do a quick change, for the idea rarely occurred to Mother before she heard the first clang of the church bell. So up to the bedroom, off with the jersey, on with the sailor suit and Sunday boots. Back downstairs, we were attacked with brush and comb, a handkerchief stuffed into one trouser pocket and a penny in the other. A final 'Look sharp now' sent us scurrying up the street the two hundred yards to church, like ambassadors doing penance for the souls of the other nine Cramps. But we needn't have hurried, for the Parson was usually late and the Verger kept ringing until he arrived.

The path from the street to the church porch was slab-stoned and slimy. To one side, a noticeboard warned of a parish meeting, long since part of history. On the other side was a majestic stone lion, crouched at the head of a young man's grave, gazing bold-eyed to the east as if ready to spring up when the last trump sounded. We walked on the grass to touch the stony head, then made for the open porch where Medowes, the Verger, pulled on the rope, and gazed at the Crown Inn opposite where the first customers were entering.

The single bell clanged dully, as if out of sorts, and seemed to convey more warning than welcome. Pigeons, disturbed from their belltower home, circled the neighbouring houses with harsh slapping wings, and out in the fields, farmers took out their watches and said, 'Parson's late again. Nowt like hard work to get yer moving.' The Verger smiled as we passed, and spat on his right hand to show he was doing a good job. Did he ring for love or money, I wondered, or did he simply relish his power, to make the village listen?

Cecil shadowed me into church and we paused by the cold marble font. The red tiled floor was damp and sticky; the place smelt of death rather than life eternal. Distantly on the altar, two candles guttered in the draught. A robin flew the length of the nave and vanished in the organ loft. Cecil, who was eight years old, whispered, 'Shall we go home?' I, being two years braver, said, 'No!' and walked slowly down the aisle. Our boots clanked on the iron grids which covered the stoves that lay below floor level. They were never lit, for it would have made no difference. The church was a barn of a place, a redbrick Victorian horror, built to impress from the outside and devoid of comfort or beauty within. Dust lay thick on most pew seats, broken here and there by a mouse run or traces of birds. Only the four front pews were clean, so we sat on the rearmost of these, and thumbed through a prayer book to pass the time. 'Not to be taken away', it said, a poor advert I thought for the quality of the customers. Cecil passed his book to me. The word 'away' had been scratched out and someone had added 'except after meals'.

But my reverie was soon disturbed by the clip-clop of a woman's footsteps. I heard them negotiate the iron grid on tiptoe and the blacksmith's daughter brushed past our pew, a cold draught in her wake. She sat in the front pew on our side and I was silently grateful; she had a clarion voice through talking to her deaf mother and, being a regular, she knew when to stand or sit. Closely behind came the Vicar, cassock skirted against the cold in the monkish tradition; and with him the Verger and the boy who pumped the organ bellows.

In a matter of seconds, the Vicar came out of his vestry and announced 'a few changes' to the order of service. We would sing first and last verses only of the hymns, and 'say', not chant, the psalms. The sermon from five feet over our heads was directed at the empty pews behind us, where ghostly listeners heard that you did not live by bread alone, though most of the world was trying to. Five minutes of this and, like a man who had issued his final warning, the Vicar spun round to the east and muttered the words which I knew always ended the sermon. But I never did hear what came after 'And now to God the Father', for from that point the Vicar's back was firmly towards the congregation.

Collection during the final hymn was taken on a silver plate with a red velvet cover. Not that our gifts would clatter so loudly as to upset the singing. It was now that

the Verger emerged as a true professional. With unhurried step he moved six pews back and collected the
plate; bearing it breast high as if already piled with
treasure, he advanced up the aisle to the blacksmith's
daughter, turned right and proffered the plate. She
paused while she finished a very high note, and then
presented her offering; three slow steps and our turn
came. I took the plate from the Verger's hand and gazed
at the silver threepence placed dead centre. Well to the
left I placed my penny and Cecil placed his on the right.
It looked more that way, I thought. On went the plate to
the boy at the blower, though whether he gave behind his
curtain, I have my doubts. On still by the longest route to
the organist and then the march to the altar, where the
Verger with sweeping mime-like action, placed his own
coin on the plate.

Our gifts were blessed, and that was that. Outside, the
world looked just the same, and I had the distinct feeling
it was warmer than the church.

PAINTED on the archway over the roodscreen in a
local church were the ten commandments. One said
that on the Sabbath, 'Thou shalt do no manner of work.'
Nor was there anything about exceptions for farmers. Yet
foddering with Father, not churchgoing, was my frequent
Sunday morning task for many years. I felt on firmer
ground with the New Testament. We could pull a bullock
from the ditch with an easy conscience, but what about
feeding and mucking out? I found it very confusing
especially as our need to work on Sunday did not stop
with animals. In summer, when there was hay about,
Father would often say, 'We'd better knock on; the glass
is dropping; can't leave good stuff to get spoilt.' So for one
reason or another up the village we'd drive in the dog-cart
on Sunday morning, with myself feeling somewhat uneasy. The working men lolled in their doorways, smoking

their 'twist' and 'shag', mostly waiting for the pubs to open. All were dressed in their Sunday attire. Boots kept for Sunday were blacked, not dubbined. Cloth trousers replaced workaday corduroys. Many who went bare necked in the week now sported a 'muffler', plain or spotted. Most men would nod as we passed, and Father responded with an almost imperceptible lift of the hand that held the reins. On up the street; turn left at the top; no need to pull on the reins. Thimble the pony knew the way, like her advance guard, the shepherd dog. She even stopped at the first farm gate where we started the morning's work.

Whatever the Sunday work might be we were expected to be home and changed by twelve thirty, the time when we sat down for dinner. Placing at table was by seniority, save that I was positioned strategically at the end, my task throughout the meal being to keep two water jugs replenished from buckets in the pantry. I had the advantage of a panoramic view of the unfolding meal, which until the very last moment was concealed in large white dishes keeping warm on hearth and hob, or in the oven. The centre of the table was clear, except for water jugs and cruet. The first sign of positive action was Father steeling the carver to razor sharpness. Then all eyes turned to the oven, and Mother swung open the door, releasing a cloud of steam and gravy fat. Expertly she transferred the vast joint from pan to oval dish, and placed it before Father who attacked it with smooth precision. Slice fell on slice as Father commented on the quality and pronounced his verdict on the butcher. This was the cue for Robert my eldest brother to open a conversation on the merits of various cattle breeds, or the possibility of running a butcher's shop as well as the farm; meanwhile, we young ones sat quietly, hands in lap. To reveal them before necessary was to risk a challenge of dirty hands or nails from sister Muriel. This would require squeezing one's way to the sink and unpopularity for the disturbance entailed. Once the meal started we were quite safe, for there were other things to occupy the company.

Serving began as Mother removed lids from vegetable dishes on the hob. What would they contain? From my end I could only guess, till the bouquet of brussels sprouts or parsnips or swedes rippled along the dark oak beams and finally enveloped me. Suddenly the flow of food in my direction began; Mother served vegetables, Muriel meat and gravy, and each full plate was passed down from hand to hand. When three were served, eating could begin, though none waited long, so smooth was the rhythm. We were fed by a secret formula known only to Mother, which presumably took account of our capacity and our need. Our likes and dislikes were irrelevant.

What with the food, the fire and eleven people, the kitchen grew steadily hotter. Mist condensed on the water jugs and steadily curtained the windows; the cat removed itself from the hearth and sprawled flat bellied on cool quarry tiles, and Mother flung back the oven door as a temporary screen. From my lowly seat I could see knives and forks rising and falling in ragged rhythm, till the first course ended. Empty plates retraced their former journey but this time were shunted to the sink, there to soak in hot water and soda.

The second course got under way with the unveiling of two boiled apple puddings. The connoisseur can remove the cloth from the basin without breaking the suet case, but the true professional, and Mother was that, can also invert the basin and discharge the pudding as a shapely whole, with juices seeping gently through the base. The distribution now became a matter of geometric accuracy, with sections neatly removed; not the hit-and-miss affair that results when an apple avalanche slides down a mountain of pastry, leaving the server to tunnel blindly into a shapeless mass. So the pudding reached us, neatly placed, and girdled with custard, not drowned in it! That was correct, said Mother, so that's what we all said, and liked it.

Lunch over, Mother and Father retired, 'to put their feet up for a few minutes', which, judging by the snores which drifted downstairs, meant two hours' solid sleep. For the rest of us, there was the golden rule: do what you like, but be quiet. Apart from those of us who were ear-marked for milking or shepherding, the rest of the day was free. Older ones dressed up for courting or visiting friends. We younger ones read in the sitting room, or in fine weather roamed over the fields or played games in the orchard.

Sunday evening had a sadness all its own. Life seemed to hover in a vacuum, awaiting the genuine pulse of Monday morning. The wan sound of distant parish bells seemed to me reminders of a lost cause as our own church so amply witnessed. Only in our two pubs did the dying embers of the week seem to glow bright. In the Cramp home, life centred on the drawing room where a day-long fire had scarcely removed the must of the previous week or aired the piano. We sat stiffly on a suite of uncut moquette and sang hymns while Mother played. Always there were the sad ones like 'Now the day is over' and 'For those in peril on the sea'. Death seemed to be dangerously close on Sundays. Sometimes we coaxed Mother to tell stories of her childhood; how her father actually built and paid for a Chapel for Primitive Methodists (I imagined them dressed in sheepskins at first), how she had to walk a mile each way to Sunday school, morning and afternoon; and how, if it was wet, she wore high boots buttoned to the knee with twelve buttons. When we registered disbelief, Mother showed us the family photograph album. But that, like the whole of Sunday, seemed totally unreal: unreal as the sight of Father clutching a crumpled Sunday paper to his chest, head lolling forward and dreaming all the time of Monday morning.

*

MONDAY was washday regardless of season or weather. At eight thirty precisely, Mrs Swingler the washerwoman arrived, full of bustle and menace. Even the dog cowered in his kennel and uttered no bark as she came up the drive. Clearly, like me, he disliked the smell of soda and soapsuds which accompanied her. She had her trade written all over her. Hands, arms, face and neck were bright pink through much standing over hot soapy water and dolly tubs. Her eyes were the colour of the blue she dangled in the rinsing water; her hair was tightly drawn back to a bob in the nape of her neck. If it ever had kink or curl, it had been steamed out long ago. But the features to which my eyes always returned were her enormous biceps, which were quite the equal of the blacksmith's.

Having deposited her coat, and drunk half a pint of heavily sweetened cocoa straight from a Toby jug, she began work. Being stone deaf, she heard not a word of the instructions Mother could not resist giving. Nevertheless, by twelve o'clock she had washed the linen of half a dozen beds, the personal clothing of eleven people, to say nothing of towels, tea cloths, tablecloths and flannels. Once she got to work it was impossible to keep track of her actions for the back kitchen was heavy with steam. The outside drain steamed and frothed over as every now and again, dirty water surged down. Sometimes one heard the rhythmic thud of dolly pegs against the corrugated sides of the washtub.

But most impressive were the heavy thuds: like giant footfalls I always thought. These came from the wringer or 'mangle' as we called it. They indicated that thick articles like blankets had been squeezed between huge wooden rollers, causing pressure weights to rise. Then suddenly as the article spilled through, the weights crashed down. 'Is her foot underneath,' I wondered when very young, 'and would a deaf woman cry out?' I need not have feared: perhaps I should say hoped. For at intervals

Mrs Swingler emerged, pinker than pink, with a clothes basket on her hip, and headed for the orchard where clothes lines ran between the apple trees. By eleven o'clock the orchard looked as if the mainmast of a full-rigged sailing ship had collapsed across it. Line props thick as spars supported sagging wires; sheets and blankets slapped harshly, and ghostly wind-filled combinations and long-johns hung like white skins whose bodies had been washed away.

Lunch on Monday was a poor attenuated thing of Irish stew and jacket potatoes followed by baked apples. By two o'clock the kitchen was safe for no man. From the open window came the heavy smell of flatiron on linen, and neat piles of clothes sprouted round the kitchen: sheets, blankets, shirts, socks, all in beautiful order. It seemed a shame they should ever be dirtied again. After tea when the washerwoman had gone home, happy with her two-shilling piece, darning began. The largest item was socks, which, being made all of wool, developed frequent holes. But thirty pairs of socks or no, the job was done — until the following Monday.

TUESDAY is market day in Market Harborough. Admission to the market is by way of a pillared gateway through which flow streams of sheep and cattle with men and dogs drawn along in their wake and several eddies of small boys. A glance forward and nearer the heart of the market reveals a chequerboard of iron-fenced islands. On some, tightly penned, are cattle, sheep and pigs. Between the islands and fed from the main gate, animal whirlpools form; then just as suddenly dissolve and flow on. Here and there iron gates acting like sluices filter animals onto new island prisons. Cattle drovers wielding gnarled ash sticks hammer on the pens and the backs of animals; they bawl animal orders in animal voices and somehow not only survive the maelstrom but bring order to it.

Yet there are some few moments when chaos really does threaten. A sow, seemingly bent on *felo de se* makes suicidal rushes until a net is thrown over her. She is towed away on her side rasping squawks of hurt pride that only a pig can give. Elsewhere a solitary steer merges with a group of fat cattle already sold and moving toward the adjacent abattoir. It will be reprieved I am sure, or someone will complain next week of tough lean meat. Sheep are so tightly packed that collie dogs run freely over their backs keeping them in an invisible cage of fear until they are suddenly penned. Overall hovers a gentleman from the RSPCA to see fair play.

Scattered across the market maze are groups of farmers in twos and threes. Some stand near the cattle they have long nurtured for sale, reluctant now to sell at any price, wedded more to their cattle than their families. Then there are some cloth-capped smallholders with leathery faces and hard muscled bodies. A good sale today could redeem them from some of the arduous piecework — hedging, thatching and ditching — with which they augment their living. Their economic survival depends on their physical strength. When this burns out they can finish in the workhouse just as easily as a common labourer unless they have a few savings or working children to fall back on.

Clearly distinguishable in the market are certain irritable and waspish men darting from group to group of farmers. These are dealers, buying and selling wherever they scent a small profit. Their chief tactic is to bemuse, cajole and bully, especially if they find a small farmer out of touch with the market. They will frighten a potential seller with tales of falling market prices and sometimes be joined by a secret accomplice who pretends to be taking a passing interest. This latter may recommend a private sale rather than risk the luck of the auction. The dealer will sometimes stuff half-a-dozen pound notes of 'luck money' in the would-be seller's pocket to persuade him to accept an offer; or seize and shake his hand violently as if the deal has been concluded; or scribble out a cheque with similar intent and thrust it into the seller's hand.

Some dealers are past-masters at selling a dozen or so cattle as a group. Such groups are usually watched over by dogs in an open area of the market. A cunning drover manoeuvres the cattle round and round seemingly to show the buyer the even quality of the group. As like as not he craftily conceals the beast with a tubercular lump on its neck or a swollen hip or one eye or some other defect. A rival bidder, a stooge of course, may chance by to add interest and speed up the action. Throughout the bargaining a battery of words is brainwashing the victim and many a small farmer falls prey to these tactics.

Away from these minor skirmishes the real battle of wits is fought out in the main auction ring. Here, on tiered benches round a central arena cluster the better-class farmers. They have come tweedily clad from the lush Midland farm lands to buy cattle for fattening that are newly arrived from Ireland and Wales. All eyes are bent on the bullocks at the centre of the ring. The farmers sit like a silent orchestra hypnotised by their auctioneer-conductor. His sharp electric voice crackles out a succession of sounds and figures which have meaning only to the initiated. Clearly he has a personal tonic-sol-fa for he races up and down his scale as if unable to find a pause. But listen carefully; let the ear grow accustomed and a glimmer of meaningful sound emerges.

'What am I bid? Fifty? Forty-five? Forty, then? Forty I'm bid. Forty, forty, forty, forty. Can I say two? One then? Give me one. Forty-one, one, one, one, one, two, two, forty-two, three, three; four, forty-four. You're out on my left. Forty-five, five, five. Six will you? Six, six, six, seven, seven, forty-seven. Eight will you make it? At forty-eight and I'm selling at forty-eight; for the last time at forty-eight.'

There is a moment of crisis as the voice pauses. Can it

really be held in check? Is the hypnotism failing? Not quite! Someone in the silent orchestra has sent a signal which triggers another explosion of words.

'It's nine, nine, nine, nine, forty-nine, forty-nine. Fill it up, gentlemen. Can I say fifty?' Obviously he can and does and in a matter of seconds his gavel crashes down on his rostrum. The spell is broken. Everyone breathes freely again. Someone has bought six bullocks at fifty pounds apiece. Yet no bidder has been heard, no head visibly nodded, no hand raised. But John Jones has bought them says the auctioneer. Nobody disputes this information. There follows a brief moment of frenetic activity in the pit. The six bullocks which till now have been driven round in a tight circle escape down a newly revealed exit. Others take their place. Once more the farmers become obedient effigies; the hypnotist has cast his spell.

Back in the town farmers' wives hunt down bargains on the market stalls. In the main the women are big handed, ampled bosomed and heavy footed, seeming to dominate the stall holders as they churn through their wares. Plucked from disordered piles are corset laces, bloomers to keep out farmhouse draughts, lisle stockings, garter elastic and darning wools; perhaps also leg rings to identify their hens and a pot egg or two to encourage them to lay, for eggs are a vital source of extra income. The amount is a closely guarded secret lest the husband reduce the housekeeping money. Groceries too must be bought including often a whole Stilton cheese; sometimes also a replacement chamber pot or two.

The wife's day finishes with a good cream tea. Husband is approaching now. He has bought well today and a drover is already halfway home with the cattle.

'Had a good day Father?'

'Well, so-so, fair to middling.'

Mother can interpret the language. There could be a new hat for her in the deal or even a winter coat. She is happy with her own purchases too. Altogether the day is without blemish. They float home in their gig with a high-stepping horse and the ostler is pleased with his sixpence.

Langton
on a Winter's Night

WESTWARD from our village after a winter sunset a different glow creeps up the night sky. It marks the place where Leicester tries to fight back the darkness as though it were an alien thing, and where townsfolk crowd to the magnet lights. Delayed sometimes in the city cattle market on a winter afternoon, I have seen their lights switch on, and been trapped in a yellow wet cocoon. Then I have felt truly benighted in a world of yellow beasts and yellow men.

If you walk in the country of a winter's afternoon between four and six o'clock, at no point can you scratch a line between night and day. Eyes adjust to a new beauty of form and presence in the landscape. In the field nearby, bullocks, now large as bison, make sounds like tearing cloth as they rip off a late supper from half-dead winter grass, before they sprawl down and enjoy their cud. But I have work to do and walk down the footpath in the direction of the western light. At the bottom of the village I must leave a message with our man Joe, then turn about, go the length of the village and leave a note with Mother's dressmaker. I am in the private world of night, so I walk slowly to enjoy it. No street lamps have invaded our privacy, but the ground is as familiar as our own kitchen floor. I've trodden it a thousand times. I know the crack between two kerb stones where I once found a whole penny, and the spot where my brother and I found a dead sparrow which we buried after holding a funeral service for it. And my journey will take me past Bucketboy Lane, where a ghost used to rattle a chain at the wellhead to warn others against an early demise. I pass the spot where an ash tree root runs like a distended vein across the footpath. I stand on it as always and rock in the dark.

The footpath suddenly ends and with it the granite kerb. Just one kick for luck! I swing my boot over the kerb edge, and the steel blakies in heel and toe send out a stream of sparks. Suddenly these are matched by a real shooting star which plunges earthwards over Mr Watts' walnut tree. But I move ahead towards a tiny orange beacon which tells where our man Joe lives with his wife and one child in a tiny cottage. There's one room and a kitchen downstairs, two tiny bedrooms upstairs and a toilet in the garden. The light comes from a candle. It still lacks a day to payday and Joe must have run out of lamp oil as usual; he's probably borrowed the half candle. No use knocking at the front door: that's permanently sealed against wind and weather with newspapers and putty, so round to the back where I call Joe by name. He opens the door long enough for me to see that he has a good log fire, and potatoes roasting on a grill hung on the front of the iron grate. He'll no doubt eat them with the beef dripping Mother gives him every week.

My message given, I turn back up the village. To my right there are lights on all over the manor house; probably a junketing to attract suitors for the daughters. Faint strands of music confirm this. Nearer at hand a light shines high up through heavy curtains. That's Mrs Bagshaw the midwife and the only cottage with a lamp that hangs from the ceiling. She takes it to confinements. It's no fun delivering babies by candlelight. It's said she also carries a hammer and nails to hang the lamp where most convenient for her work. Close by is the house of 'Chinnerman' Cox who works at the manor. His one and only room is in darkness but uncurtained. When he and his wife go to bed in winter he takes the old plush curtains off their rod to add warmth to the bed. Tomorrow he'll be cleaning up the mess after the manor party. Father says that's what makes socialists.

Now I can see under the archway leading to the premises of Mr Z. Busby, carpenter. Wagons in a crumpled laager stand round in various stages of repair. Some, bare ribs silhouetted against the night sky, need new cladding; some, wheelless, rest like giant coffins on blocks. In a nearby shed I know stand the sections of real coffins, seasoning against the day of need. I wonder if Zacharias has one ready for himself. And whose turn will be next? Before long I have two possible answers to this question. First, there's old Mrs Jelly who lives on her own. Her asthma is so bad I can hear her wheezing as I pause near her door which opens onto the footpath. Her room is dark; she's probably asleep on her sofa because she can't lie flat. If I remind Mother, she'll send her some honey and blackcurrant purée tomorrow.

My reflections are drowned by George Bailey, pensioner and ex-farmworker, as he tacks an uneasy course from pub to home. Knowing the perils of the kerb on his right, he cannons off the hedges and fences on his left. God-guided, he arrives at his own front door and flops down on a mounting stone left over from the days when his house was a pub. He'll enter shortly: it takes courage now. His wife died a month ago, the first of our usual spate of winter deaths. George is alone in the world. Next year or the year after it will be the workhouse for him and shortly after that, one of those coffins nearby. Few country people survive long in the workhouse. What has immobility between clean sheets in a hothouse atmosphere to do with the world they have known? Broken hearts soon make broken bodies.

In a shaft of light from the police sergeant's house, I can see that the footpath is glistening white with hoar frost, so I move to the road which is rougher and safer. Suddenly, a door opens in the house of a widowed and childless smallholder. He's in a bad way of things and may have to sell his small farm and become a landless labourer. But he still maintains his Christian faith. At the

Uncle's threshing machine in Northants

Father in the pony float

Mother with the Author on her right and his brother Cecil in 1926

The Village Street

Tea with our backs to a cob of hay. The Author in the centre, aged 17, with his father on his right

moment he is posting a letter. Then he'll move down the village to meet his lady friend. They are twin pillars of the chapel though crumbling fast say some. Nightly they meet combining pleasure with planning concerts, tea-parties, picnics and other ground bait to lure a diminishing congregation, but the final catch is small.

Outside the police house is a thirty-foot yew shaped to fine topiary and surmounted by a cock. The moon has risen over a hill to the north so I wait till the cock sits inside the golden ring before moving on to Spinney Lane. This leads to an old sand quarry where fir trees now grow. Being dry, sheltered, and dark, it is favoured by courting couples. Sometimes on a winter's night young boys creep to the lip of the tree-dark quarry and listen. But they fear to enter and so never divine the secrets of their elders. Occasionally, they challenge the darkness and send a stone crashing down amongst the trees, but then race home to escape retribution from those youths who are 'courting strong' and sometimes emerge to defend their honour against younger brothers.

On past the post office, squat, thatched and now silver-grey in the moonlight. There stands the postbox, day and night open mouthed, waiting to gobble up the village secrets. And only the postman has a key to its belly. His work is confidential but he's also human. He knows what letters make lovers weep and debtors tremble. He knows when daughters away in service write to their mothers in the sloping oval hand taught in the village school. And he knows when distraught mothers send postal orders to wayward daughters, instead of the other way round.

Further up the street I reach the house of a rich farmer and cattle dealer. Drink in the furtherance of business has reduced his estate and ruined his health. Once a man of power and influence, his master is now a slim white-coated nurse. For a moment as I pass, she slides open the sash window to freshen the room. But her patient bawls a protest that echoes over half the village, and down comes the window with a thud.

Peace reigns over the blacksmith's house. I imagine his vast and muscled body sleeping like Hercules after his labour. The shoeing shop stands open to the night, tingeing the air with an odour of ammonia and burnt hoof. The noise of his trade is locked inside anvil and hammer, and the spark of his forge awaits tomorrow's breath, but there are sounds of life abundant emanating from the Crown Inn. Snug and public bar must both be crowded: obviously a skittle match against men from a neighbouring village. I have never crossed the threshold of The Crown, but our man Joe has described the interior many a time. Here of an evening with his half pints of mild and bitter resting on upturned barrels for tables, he lives out his fantasy life. By ten o'clock, judging from reports of other villagers, he is a prince among men; our sheepdog has become a prizewinning collie; Thimble, the pony, can not only unhasp a gate with her nose (which she really does) but can pick a lock with her teeth, and Joe himself can strip a cow of three gallons of milk in six minutes. Standing opposite The Crown now, I too am ready to let my imagination be stirred. The pub door opens briefly. No human customer leaves, but a belch of noise, light and smoke propels a shape into outer darkness. As the pub door opens yet again, I recall the wallpainting of hellfire in a local church. There is a momentary vision of tormented wraiths among smoke and dancing lights, till suddenly, the devil whom I cannot see pitches another soul out into eternal night. This last victim turns out to be Reg Hooper. With empty pocket and full belly he edges homeward past the War Memorial stopping to make water by the churchyard wall. Tonight he cares not one jot that engraved on the granite plaque of the memorial are the names of his three brothers.

As I draw towards the baker's house, the rising moon has dusted it with flour. Upstairs I know sleeps Mr Freestone, a widower now, but wedded still to his bread. There he lies, as always I'm sure, with flour in his ears, his eyebrows and his hair. To give us our daily bread he'll rise at four o'clock, but few who handle his warm and punchy loaves at ten o'clock will ever give that a thought. The church lying opposite the bakery stirs in me the thought that if Jesus' father hadn't been a carpenter, he should have been a baker, selling bread, which in our village is life to so many.

The church darkens the southern sky and casts a moon shadow on the houses beneath it. In God's name the inhabitants have enough shadows without this. Two Burton families live in adjacent cottages, sixteen souls in all. The parents must know their own families but no one else can sort them out. Two weekly wages amounting to about seventy shillings keeps the lot of them. Perhaps their proximity to the bakehouse helps their survival, for the baker is 'soft as dough' and allows huge debts to build up. The Burton children look tough as nails despite snotty noses winter and summer. They must sleep several to a bed. More likely they sleep on the floor, and it's rumoured they've broken through to the roof space and some sleep there in summer. A smell of fried onions drifts through a missing window pane; perhaps the secret of health is onions. But they are not too poor to keep a pet, for suddenly a door opens, and somebody curses and shoe-toes a cat into the street. Their several years of plenty will come, as the children grow to school-leaving age, start work, and pay well for their keep. The greatest beneficiary will probably be the publican. But who can blame the parents for seeking the comfort of his Snug where you not only drink hops but breathe them, where you can enjoy a good spit into the fire without half-a-dozen children trying to copy you, and where there's always a chance of a 'towny' dropping in and standing treat for a pint.

My reverie is disturbed by a cat rubbing round my ankles. I recognise that it belongs to Robbo, the recluse

with no visible means of subsistence. It is said he keeps
the cat because in the spring it catches and brings home
young rabbits. The less charitable say he also fries and
eats the rats and mice it brings.

Outside the house of a gentleman farmer, two youths
are lounging in the darkness; but not aimlessly, because as
I draw level I hear they are in converse with servant girls
through the pantry window. Perhaps the girls know that
the way to a country lad's heart is through his stomach.

At the top of the village I skirt an ancient mud wall. It
is honeycombed with holes in which during the summer
live solitary bees. But of more immediate concern to me,
the wall surrounds a farmyard belonging to the gentleman
aforesaid. In one of the barns is a loft where it is rumoured
cockfighting sometimes takes place. The birds, apparently,
are brought ready trained from stockingers who work in a
nearby factory town. For a moment I think I can see a
light through a roof window in the barn, but it turns out
to be only the reflected moonlight.

I come to the end of my errand now and walk down the
path to the dressmaker's cottage. No lights show within,
but I am a silver messenger in a silver moonlit world. The
door opens before I reach it. Miss Brown must have been
sitting at her window seat, looking out at the beautiful
world of night. I collect the parcel and trot home. If I'm
too long, there will be questions; and how can I talk about
the world of my dreams?

Shear Sheep, Make Hay, Kill Pig

IN THE 1920s many of the animal medicines now available were unknown. In any case, most farmers I knew preferred to doctor their own animals rather than risk the expense of calling a vet — in our case from five miles away. In consequence, some farmers suffered heavy stock losses. Father, however, was skilled with sick animals, especially milking cows and breeding ewes. Normal healthy sheep will weather all sorts of hardship out of doors. But once they need to be brought in for any kind of treatment, they soon go off their feed, become faint-hearted and die. Cows, by contrast, will endure pain with great fortitude and are good patients.

Difficult lambing cases were Father's speciality. Having tiny and, despite hard work, sensitive hands, he was much in demand for difficult deliveries. He was adept at turning a lamb that was 'coming wrong' and, if a ewe did need sewing up after a difficult delivery, he was as skilful as a surgeon. I acted as his assistant in many a draughty barn. Our stock-in-trade was disinfectant and warm water for our hands and the ewe's hind parts; and for sewing up a ewe that had 'put its body out', a thin curved bodkin and long white laces which were made for ladies' bodices.

Whenever a ewe died leaving orphan lambs, we began the tricky process of 'hanging on', that is, inducing another ewe which had a full 'bag' of milk and only a single lamb, to adopt the newcomer. The first reaction of the foster mother is usually rejection and, left alone with the orphan, she will sometimes butt it to death. The great secret to secure acceptance is to get a quantity of the ewe's milk through the new lamb's system, by restraining her while he sucks. After a couple of days, when he goes to suck, and mother sniffs the wagging tail, he has the acceptable scent. Some farmers smeared the lamb with the ewe's urine, but our method, though time-consuming, was usually successful.

When a healthy ewe lost a lamb and we wanted her to adopt another, we used a different technique. First we found an orphan from a neighbouring farmer. The dead lamb was carefully skinned and his wet skin fastened on the newcomer, usually by putting it over his back and making four slits for his legs. This method conveyed the right scent to the mother. One problem resulted. Adoption took several days, by which time our little lamb was quite dependent on his second coat. Suddenly to deprive him of it would mean a chill and possibly pneumonia. Hence the skin remained in place but periodically the 'hem' was trimmed until one sunny day we would remove the final remnant. The process of reduction meant first catching your lamb. Being fleet of foot, the task usually fell to us boys.

In lambing time it was not unusual to go downstairs for breakfast and find two or three lambs occupying pride of place on the rug before the kitchen fire. These had lambed in the night and become starved, often because the ewe's milk had not yet begun to flow. Father's recipe for revival was a teaspoonful of brandy in warm cow's milk. The effect was startling, and they were soon staggering to their feet and bleating. If they made water on the hearth-rug, there was no complaint from mother. All was forgotten where survival of livestock was concerned.

At week-ends my job was often to keep an eye on the lambing ewes in the home paddock. They seemed to lamb in bursts. One minute the ewes were grazing happily; the next moment several had separated from the main flock, moved to hedge or protective hurdle shelter, and started to 'strain'. Most lambed without help and stayed out of doors. But there were the normal problems, including lambs born dead or with rickets, or sometimes a freak lamb like one we had born with two heads.

At night, ewes still to lamb were brought into a smaller enclosure and visited at twelve, two, and four o'clock. As a teenager, I often did the first shift on Saturday night, doing school homework to pass the time. If there were problems, Father was called.

Our very young lambs had two main enemies: foxes and crows. Fortunately the fox usually selected a weakling which had tucked itself under a hedge or in a hollow for warmth and allowed its mother to wander away. The fox would crush the neck and drag the lamb away without trace. Only a bleating ewe was there to remind one of the loss. To deter foxes we painted every newborn lamb with 'fox-oil'. Though evil-smelling, it never affected the ewe's attention to her lamb. Occasionally carrion crows and magpies made vicious attacks, especially when they had young to feed. They would peck the eyes out of a sleeping or sickly lamb, then rip open the soft belly and tear out the entrails for their brood. In a hard winter, magpies searching for sheep ticks on a sheep's back would sometimes peck too deep and draw blood. Relishing the taste they would rip savagely at the flesh and leave raw wounds.

Periodically throughout the lambing season the new lambs had to be 'doctored', while still young. This meant cutting off the tails of all lambs, leaving a two-inch stump, and castrating the male lambs at the same time. Anyone who has witnessed these operations will be amazed at how quickly most lambs recover from the surgery. Twenty-four hours later, they show no sign of their ordeal. We always removed the tails with a knife: blood quickly congealed on the wound. During the following evening we always checked for bleeding. If there was a problem we bandaged the tail lightly; according to Father, a piece of 'fuzz-ball' strapped on the wound was the old remedy.

Some farmers used a hot iron to sever the tail, but with no better results than our own.

News of any major event on the farm was usually known in advance in the village through 'our man'. Hence no sooner were the lambs' tails off than one or two older inhabitants, who knew what a delicacy they were, collected enough for several pies. The tails were first scalded to remove the wool, then cooked slowly in a pie under thick pastry. It was these same folk who appeared whenever we had a cow newly calved. The first rich milk or 'beestings' could not go into the churn, and it was too much even for a calf left with the mother. Hence we gave quantities away. It made the most delicious custard without any additions, and quite often had to be diluted with water.

When sheep, lambs or cattle died from any cause other than virulent disease, their final resting-place was with the village knackerman. He collected the carcasses in a deep-sided tumbril-like cart into which the curious could not see except from their bedroom windows. Needless to say, folk knew the rumble of this particular cart and rushed upstairs to view the latest casualty and often to pronounce judgement on the owner. On the village outskirts was a piggery where the flesh was fed to pigs after being boiled in giant cauldrons.

The nearest a farmer comes to robbery with violence must surely be when shearing his sheep. One minute the ewe stands, a matronly figure, square-backed, full-bellied and wearing a coat three inches thick, oily with lanolin, proof against wind and rain. Five minutes later she looks a poor white painted thing, fragile, spindle-legged and half the size; robbed of her fleece, naked as the day she was born, a creature undone, like a lady in an evening gown who has suddenly lost her mink wrap. The assault on nature is brief. The ewe is flung on her side, a leg pressed over her neck to restrain her protests, and shearing begins.

Our man was no professional shearer. This once-a-year

job meant an amateur approach and the sheep suffered accordingly. Some emerged in a bloody mess, nicked in a dozen places, usually on the soft underbelly. Ointment was smeared on the worst wounds, but mainly the sheep took their chance. As the shearer plunged the cutting head under the fleece, the wool lifted off in a milk-white froth, slashed here and there with scarlet as blades took too fine a cut, when the ewe kicked wildly, resenting the plunder. By the end of the day the shearer was soaked in the oil of scores of fleeces; clothes shone greasy wet like the skin of a snake in sunlight, and grimy hands grew soft and lily-white.

Slung between two trees in the orchard and close by the shearing pen hung a giant hessian bag. Into its belly Father stuffed each rolled fleece, till by day's end it resembled a bulging ship's hull with masts at either end.

It fell to me often to brand the shorn sheep, a most satisfying job. Dip the iron in thin warm tar, stab it on the pearly white flank, and the sheep belongs to HCC. Soon, scattered over the paddock, were two hundred ewes all bearing the same emblem. We had our initials burnt on the shafts of our tools, and even the ladders and wheelbarrows; we blazoned our name on carts and wagons and now the sheep flaunted it too. As they streamed up the village street, on the way to the main farm, doors opened to admire the strange white pageant, and cottagers' voices echoed 'HCC'.

WHEN JUNE came in, the whole family showed an extraordinary interest in the barometer. We tapped the glass as often as we passed it, and grumbled if it was not at 'Change' and moving up. We tried to exert moral pressure on God by insisting among ourselves that the weather must take up in June if we were to have hay worth the getting. And when the barometer rose and the sun still didn't shine, we felt the Almighty had cheated.

But, still acting in good faith, we prepared the mowing machine. We dragged it from the nettles that always invaded the machine shed, with scant thought for the brood of mice which we usually found in a nest of chewed hay in the mower toolbox. We oiled the machine, sharpened the knives and waited. In fact, the whole district waited, for, over the years, so great was the respect for Father's knowledge and intuition that other farmers took their cue from him.

I still recall the shock I experienced (and I can only have been ten or eleven) when one Saturday late in June Father was missing from his accustomed armchair at breakfast. Despite nine other people being seated, there seemed to be a hole in the kitchen, for, from my remote seat, I realised that my view of the fire was not totally obscured. I could even see the flames. Mother soon cleared up the mystery. Father had risen at five o'clock, journeyed to the main farm and 'put the mower in'. At eight o'clock, I took his breakfast, driving fast in horse and float, to keep it warm; fried gammon between two tin plates, resting on a hot brick in a box, plus half a gallon of tea.

When I arrived at the field, I could see no sign of life, but I heard clearly the clack-clack of the mower. Then suddenly it rounded a bend and I could see two nodding heads with white blazes moving rhythmically up and down as the horses pushed their shoulders into the collars with even effort. Father's blue eyes twinkled as he halted beside me; his face had the joy and intensity of a man who had been first in a gold rush. I knew that in his mind's eye he could already see stack on stack of hay, breaking the field horizons. As I left him to his breakfast, I heard the distant wail of the hooter at the glue factory, five miles away. 'Are you glad you don't live in a town?' queried Father and I didn't need to answer.

For days on end in the hayfield, I sat on a horse-drawn swath-turner, flicking the hay over and over, to 'make' thoroughly. The skylarks seemed unperturbed at my repeated attack on their environment and rose from my path, singing and soaring. In the heat of the afternoon, I rode in a cloud of dust and pollen, as the twirling tines churned the hay over. Flecks of white lather rose around the horse's collar, and always by three o'clock my thoughts turned more and more to the delights of tea.

Now hayfield tea has qualities unique to its situation. Ours, two gallons of it, arrived at the field in a large conical tin can, the lid being pressed on with a seal of brown paper. But by the time the pony had jogged from home to hayfield, the slip-slopping tea had borrowed the paper's bouquet. Then, as we sat drinking with our backs to a hay-cob, the tea seemed to absorb the fragrance of the maturing hay, until I could imagine I was drinking a sort of essence of hayfield. Tiny grasshoppers, little larger than a pinhead, landed in everyone's cup. But not all of us bothered to distinguish them from the tea leaves, or hook them out with a stem of hay. It took at least two cups of tea to reveal that under the dust and pollen our lips were still pink. And only then did we start on the lettuce sand-wiches and rock-cakes.

Some half-hour later, our man Joe would rise to his feet, to make a virtue of necessity. Knowing that if he didn't say it, Father would, he stretched his arms and remarked, 'Better get started before we lose heat.' All knew what he meant. Sit too long and you stiffen up. So back to work till the rising dew stained our boots. Then home to milk the cows as the evening star shone over their mangers.

Hayfield tea was once nearly my undoing. Living in the village for a few years was an ex-naval man named Bowles who owned a powerful telescope. His great pastime was to walk the lanes on fine days and examine the surrounding countryside from different vantage points. He would report on the activities of farmers in neighbouring parishes, keep an eye on strangers as they moved through the neighbourhood, spot stray cattle on the roads and explain the origin of every puff of smoke within miles. It was also said he watched courting couples and had special night glasses. During one haytime he did me an unusual service. I had driven home from the hayfield, with our pony, Thimble, pulling the float, to fetch the tea for the workers. On returning to the field, the men were not quite ready, so I left Thimble to graze, still harnessed to the float. She could do nothing worse than knock down a hay-cob, but even this was unlikely; she was very intelligent between shafts. If a cart wheel found an obstacle she would stop immediately, back off and gently try again. At the shout of 'tea-up' I turned to fetch Thimble but she was nowhere to be seen. I climbed the ladder near the haystack and scanned the field, but no horse. In some panic now, and urged on by thirsty men, I set off running along the road back home. After some half mile, I was amazed to see Thimble being driven towards me at a steady trot by Bowles, who stopped as he drew level. 'Saw her leave the field,' he said proudly. 'Nobody aboard so I went to meet her. Stopped like a Christian when I shouted ahoy. And, by the way, there's a drop of tea missing from the urn; not Thimble's fault: I always wanted to try hayfield tea.'

The hay mellowed and matured in large cobs. As they stood along the skyline, they resembled a miniature Stonehenge. In a way, they were just as much a testament to our faith as the blocks of stone were to the men of pre-history. We believed that as we sowed, so we should reap, and that the world was a better place for what we did. We believed that 'seed time and harvest shall not fail', for we believed in a future, in this world and the next.

When would the cobs be ready to stack? Father plunged his arm into several, sniffed, and pronounced it good. So one by one the mellow heaps were dragged to the stack by a chain around their base. Each left behind a yellow circle of sun-starved grass.

Stacking hay is testing for even the strongest man. Look at the ridge of any stack, and wonder how it was built, thirty feet up, in the days when there were no machine aids. Men perched at intervals up the ascending roof relayed the hay, forkful by forkful, to the man who was capping the ridge. Through the heat of the day they worked, sweat-drenched, in the lee of the stack. Every forkful up meant a shower of hayseeds down, into the hair, shirt and socks, there to stick and chafe. Father drove his men hard, often late into the evening. I have seen the moon rise over the stack, till Father on the ridge seemed to hold the golden ball on the end of his fork and, silhouetted against the moon, he looked demonic and seemed to walk in space. I have seen strong men grow silent, too tired to talk, and heard the distant clock strike ten. And sometimes after stints like this, Father was known to utter a few words of praise. 'A pretty fair effort! Yes, pretty fair.' And then more directly to the men, 'Of course the pubs will be closed by now, but that's just as well, because we still have to milk the cows.'

Not all seasons were good. The worst summer I remember brought a twofold loss. Hay stacked damp will grow hot and fire by spontaneous combustion, as everyone knows who has felt the heat generated by a heap of green lawn clippings. One of our stacks had been none too dry, so we left hollow 'chimneys' to take out the heat. But a week later an excited boy banged on the kitchen door one evening, to say the stack was on fire. We found it well alight, but burning from the outside, inwards, and so clearly a manmade fire. In a ditch nearby the police found an old pram of the sort used by tramps to carry their goods. The parish union workhouse recognised it as belonging to a 'dosser' they had lately sheltered, and he was caught at the next workhouse on his travels. He had slept by the stack, gone to sleep smoking, and fled when he saw the results, but not before dumping his pram. Father's honour was saved: not a fire caused by stacking wet hay!

With the unsettled season came thunderstorms. Shepherding one morning we found twelve dead sheep. They had moved to a tall hedge for shelter and stood with wet backs under a barbed wire fence. Lightning travelling along it had killed them instantly. One or two still sat, natural as life, save that their heads had dropped forward. Insurance covered the loss, but the knackerman was the chief gainer.

HAY HARVEST wasn't all work for me and my brothers, and we still found time to explore the countryside. We robbed wild bees of their honey, and sucked it straight from the comb. When really hungry once, we ate pigeons' eggs raw; we made a hole at either end and sucked the contents. If there was no water to quench our thirst, we chewed 'sour grass' or green crab apples. Cowslips were abundant in our area and we gathered them for Granny to make wine. The nests and eggs of crows and magpies we ruthlessly destroyed, for these birds killed our spring lambs. There were always wasps' nests in the muckheaps, and for excitement we burnt them out with straw. One day we found a young pigeon tied by a leg to its platform-nest. Labourers sometimes did this, leaving the mother to feed the chick until it was fat enough for the pot. We dammed a stream on the farm, and taught ourselves to swim; drank mud in the effort, and grew bleary-eyed; to dry we rolled in the grass. The meadows were rich in butterflies which we learned to preserve and identify with the aid of an interested chemist friend. We knew the names and habits of every kind of bird. We noted how the linnet used horsehair to line her nest, how the wren used moss and wool, and the magpie anything he could lay his beak on, including silver paper from the workmen's cigarette packets, and binder twine stolen from the barn.

Very occasionally, purpose eluded us, and like tired dogs we flung ourselves down by a hedgerow. But challenge was always near and soon we were neck-high in nettles, standing in a ditch and cracking off elder stems, thick as your thumb. Pocket knives out, we cut six-inch sections, whittled out the pith and made ourselves whistles.

On one long trek in the late afternoon, we discovered a barn that grew out of a hillside, gaunt like a castle. At a cautionary distance below its walls we whistled shrill with our fingers; with never a falter the walls shrilled back. We questioned them loudly and back rolled disembodied voices that questioned us. We cursed them and in sepulchral tones; they echoed us but with double menace. Then suddenly night came floating in on the back of a first chill wind and we fled from the barn and its lost soul voices, in fear at our own creations. Galloping home we stared in the face of the purpling sun till retinal images like fairy balloons danced lightly ahead.

WHEN I was fifteen, I was five feet eleven inches tall, measured against the barn door, where notch after notch, each with a pencilled date, testified to my rapid growth. Like most growing boys, my thoughts dwelt often on food, and the abundance which Christmas provided was a warming prospect. The period of great plenty began with the late November pig killing. The exact time depended on the weather, the first killing coinciding with the first really cold snap. The second came in mid-December; and, when the family were all at home, there was a third in late January. So from November onwards, apart from renewing the larder with hams and bacon, we enjoyed all those delicacies which the pig so abundantly provides.

The November killing was really a sign to the whole village that Christmas was on the horizon. Forewarning of the event was spread abroad by our man who frequented The Crown Inn, and speculation began as to which villagers might participate in the spoils. Everybody knew there would be 'a little something' for the sick, the old or the very needy; also for anyone who had rendered us any special service during the year.

The pig sticking was a piece of primordial ceremonial. We really meant no harm to the pig. It was just that it happened to be the central figure in the drama. Much care had been lavished on him, to bring him up to sixteen or eighteen score pounds and now, we thought, he should be almost as proud as we were, that such pleasure for us should ensue from the final act. The killing was done by a butcher from Kibworth, two miles distant. He arrived soon after breakfast in a pony-drawn float and was greeted with the formality due to one of his special skill, and regaled with beer, bread and cheese. Then from his float came the mysterious items of his near priestly craft: a cratch, a thin rope, a bucket with a lid, bristle scrapers and a jute bag with an assortment of knives. The cratch, a sort of sacrificial altar it seemed to me, was a low, wooden, four-legged, stretcher-like affair with handles at each corner. The pig, which had been fasted throughout the previous day, was in no mood to co-operate with those who had again brought him no food. Protesting loudly, he was pulled by ears and tail to the cratch in the barn. I always thought it unfortunate for the pig world that they were so badly endowed with means by which man could handle them: no long hair to grasp, no horns to provide leverage, and a body so contoured that it is well nigh impossible to gain a grip on it with hand or rope. Hence the ignominy of the pig's last minutes. Once alongside the low cratch, it was easy to roll the pig onto the platform; there on his side he was amazingly helpless, while a rope secured him to the four handles.

By this point, lured by the squealing, one or two village folk had assembled. They would speculate on the pig's condition and weight: a sort of vested interest one might suppose. Was it equal to last year's number one killing? Had our man done a good job feeding it or was there too much fat? And it was at this point, that we, the family, sometimes recalled a minor disaster some years earlier. We had lost one pig: it had escaped, wandered into a stable and got kicked to death by a horse. To replace it, Father bought a fat pig in the market. The awful truth emerged after the killing, at the cutting up stage. The carcass didn't smell right and when we sampled the first piece of meat, the reason was all too clear. The pig had been fattened on fishmeal and was tainted. Salting improved matters a little, but much of the pig was given away and we never bought another fat pig.

To resume the story of our home-fed animal, the time of final despatch came. In one swift and easy thrust the butcher slit the pig's throat and the blood gushed into the bucket in rhythmic squirts. The squealing rapidly grew raucous and feeble; soon the pig was pronounced dead and the bleeding complete. What happened to the blood I never knew. It was the butcher's perquisite. Some said it went into black puddings: others into manure. Willing hands now seized the cratch, one man per corner and the pig was carried down to the back kitchen in a sort of triumphal procession. As it passed the living kitchen there was a pause for Mother to cast her eye over this potential source of a hundred breakfasts and much more besides. In the back kitchen the copper gurgled so rapidly that the room was dense with steam. Once inside the men moved about like wraiths, prompted occasionally by Father. On his order the hair scraping began. Water just off the boil was ladled over the pig while the scrapers removed the bristles with a harsh rasping sound. The pig gradually took on a pinker hue. Finally, a slit was made in each back leg just above the hock, a rope was passed through and the pig was suspended from a hook above the back kitchen door. Here after gutting it hung in the cool air until late afternoon when the flesh was set and the butcher returned for the cutting up.

During the winter evenings preceding the killing we young ones listened while Mother and Father discussed which gifts of meat should be disbursed and to whom. Service during the previous year was always rewarded even though it might already have been paid for in cash or kind. Also, what Father considered 'decent conduct' was acknowledged. Who then was finally included? Jones for sweeping our chimneys; Larkin the roadman whose handiwork we witnessed daily at close quarters; Baker for returfing Grandfather's grave; Mrs Swingler for doing the Monday washing; Mrs Bagshaw for midwife services to Mother for several of us though the youngest of us was of school age now; the police sergeant for his zeal in keeping poachers off the farm; Simons because he had fought in the Boer War and Father believed in the merits of Empire; Rogers, the blacksmith who shod horses thirty times a year for us without causing one to walk lame because of a tight shoe or a badly placed nail; Mrs Ward who kept the post office and by virtue of her job relayed to Father vital bits of information which, as Father said, it paid him to know; Freestone the baker for supplying us with our daily bread; Mrs Jelly because she had asthma and some good pork dripping would 'oil her tubes'. And so it went on.

The gifts varied subtly as to quality and quantity. The humblest gift was home-rendered lard or 'scratchings', those little nutty lumps left behind after the rendering of the lard. Ranking slightly higher were tripe, pig's chaps (cheeks) and 'trotters'. More rewarding cuts were a few chops, a pork pie, pig's liver and haslet. Each gift was wrapped in greaseproof paper and delivered on a white plate. Thus was the mutuality of village life recognised.

The main cutting up completed, all the meat was transferred to the cold pantry and placed on long low brick thralls. Detailed work now followed. The belly was cleaned out and placed in brine; the pig's head was split and the tongue removed; the trotters, valued for their special flavour, were removed. Fat was cut out for rendering into lard and stored in great earthenware pancheons; lean meat cut from the ribs for making into pork pies. And so for several days the great pig festival continued. Meals took on a new dimension, with liver, haslets, loin of pork, tripe, pork pies and all those titbits long vanished in the interests of 'good commercial practice'. Nothing was wasted. Even the bladder was rescued to be inflated and serve temporarily for us boys as a football, till it became too dry, cracked and burst.

Father presided over the 'mystery' of pork pie making. Regularly each year we lost the recipe, handed down in the family for generations. Regularly Father discovered it deep in the bowels of his bureau, among land titles and tithe records. Annually, it became less decipherable, as the folded paper cracked along the seams. No one thought of making a copy. It was as if only the magic of the original recipe would produce the desired result. So annually we pored over the hidden secrets, divined the message and produced pork pies whose excellence I, and no doubt others, still remember.

The vital task of salting the bacon was also Father's job. It seemed to me to resemble embalming. Armed with salt and saltpetre, he would vanish into the pantry every evening for several weeks, like a high priest entering his holy of holies; there he performed his ritualistic rubbing. Only he, by some sixth sense, knew when the curing was just right and the hams and flitches ready to adorn the walls and beams of the kitchen, there to dry off completely, against the day of eating.

Daily we lived with the fruits of our labours. When we looked on the bacon in the kitchen, the hay in the rickstead, the milk in the churns, the apples in store, our morale was uplifted. Like the great Creator, we looked on our handiwork and it was good. The townsman might look down on us, his country cousins, but we pitied him. Tied too closely to a money economy, he lost half the joy of living, we thought. Paper money only, as a reward for labour, is truly but 'a promise to pay' — and one that is never fully redeemed.

Special Occasions

ONE DAY towards the end of 1918, I was standing
where the ruts that invade our drive after winter
storms join the necklace of potholes we call the Main
Street, watching a village miracle. Jack Bolton, a boy of
my own age renowned for attempting the impossible, had
just declared that if he ran fast enough through the
puddles, the water would fly out sideways and he would
emerge dryfooted. I bet him a bull's eye mint that he
wouldn't. I had no mint, but the challenge was never
decided, for Jack, having stayed the course, refused to
give proof by removing his shoes. Our altercation came to
an end when Harry Smith, an excitable boy with eyes
perpetually ablink, came roaring down the street shouting,
'Armist-is-declared an' our dad's comin' home with a
medal.' From this I gathered that the war had ended.

Now I wasn't quite sure this was a good thing for I'd
heard Father say it took a good war to put farmers on their
feet, pity though it was. Then again, I had discovered
certain dreadful war secrets which made me feel mighty
important. The trouble was I couldn't tell anyone to
prove my importance. I did, however, tell brother Cecil
one night in bed, but not before he swore the terrible
oath of secrecy, 'This finger wet, this finger dry; cut my
throat if I tell a lie.' The secrets were, that we fattened a
little porker for the schoolmaster who paid us well for this
supplement to his rations. Also we supplied a police
inspector with rolled oats for his own pig. Furthermore,
Father had removed some of our bacon flitches from the
kitchen to the attic, because if certain people saw them
they'd feel 'bolshie' and might burn our stacks down or
something terrible.

Peace took away my secrets and we brought the bacon

down from the attic. The price of hay dropped when the army stopped buying. Father said people had been on rations so long that their guts had shrunk and they'd never need as much beef as in the old days. The schoolmaster announced we had had the last of our special holidays for potato picking, blackberrying for jam for soldiers, and gleaning corn for his hens. Altogether, peace presented a dismal prospect. There was a moment of special interest when my eldest brother Robert came home from the war, though I was scarcely aware he had gone. There was a moment of panic when he stepped into the kitchen, for Mother thought he might be lousy. But all was well and we had a special lunch. Robert insisted on eating all courses off the same plate to show how they had lived in the army. Next day he began work on the farm as usual.

Much later, when I'd almost forgotten the war and its benefits, my view of peace was considerably improved by talks of a great celebration. I heard of plans for a tea party so enormous it would have to be held in Johnson's meadow. The whole village would go, even old Mrs Jelly who was wheezed up with asthma; there would be a special tent for the likes of her. Not even rain would stop the fun and barns were earmarked just in case. Collections to foot the bill began. Father gave an unprecedented five pounds, seeing how Robert had been spared to work on the farm again, and half a dozen of us younger ones would no doubt 'eat our whack' at the celebration tea.

The day of the Peace celebrations dawned fine, and preparations consumed the morning. Cartloads of tents, flags and ropes, chairs and trestle tables, food and drink manoeuvred up Johnson's lane to the field appointed. A swarm of ragamuffin boys with nothing better to do swirled round the carts. We, of course, were forbidden such fripperies though we eyed them from a distance. One boy broke briefly away from a magnet load of food to inform me he was eating no lunch the better to do justice to tea. I personally had never found one meal an obstacle to another.

By three o'clock the village was practically empty; true someone stayed behind briefly to ring a sort of victory peal on the one and only church bell. And old Mrs Tookey was too frail to go so was left with her daughter. But they were taken a special tea in a clothes basket; a sort of Noah's ark, two of everything, that lasted several days. Old folk were transported by horse and trap, placed in an open-sided marquee and liberally plied with tea and cucumber sandwiches. I had never seen folk so human. Albert Norman, an irascible farmer, suddenly and for no obvious reason, dished out sixpences to every boy in his vicinity. Old Mrs Cooper, who had lost three sons in the war, wept with a mixture of pride, sorrow and satisfaction when she was given a place of honour close to the high-flying union jack. A crate of Guinness soon consoled her (she never drank tea and ate very little). Every labouring man had two free pints of best bitter beer, drawn from a barrel on the back of a wagon. Even 'Prodder' Wilson, a loud-mouthed labouring man, vetted his vocabulary for the occasion, and replied civilly when complimented on his medals. The Lord of the Manor made an opening speech inviting us all to make up for four years of living on rations. I thought myself quickly out of that sad state and did my duty as ordered. Knee-deep in buttercups, I queued with the other boys and caught the infection of hunger. First we were given a large paper bag, then paraded past tables laden with sandwiches. We took one from each pile and built our own conglomerate pyramid in the bag. Fish, flesh and fowl, all went in, and a capping of buns at the end. Then a large mug of tea and down on the grass to celebrate Victory. Jackie Barlow dossed down on a cowclot, gave his trousers to an attendant woman and sat barebummed in the clover. Nobody bothered! We'd won the war to end all wars, so we were told, and this was the meal of a lifetime.

For a few minutes after tea had ended, we boys sprawled pot-bellied on the grass, in the way young animals do. Then, energy restored, we agitated for action, sports, and prizes. The organisers took their cue. We raced two-legged and three-legged, frontwise and backwards, in sacks and out of them. We raced against hazards of ridge and furrow, molehills and cattle dung; and everybody won a prize, if only a bar of chocolate. But racing exhausts a boy, so cake and ginger pop to see us home, and a final present of a Peace mug. 'For King and Country', the legend said, and I was sure I had helped to win the war.

What the adults did on that glorious afternoon, I can't justly remember, though I recollect Father sidling across the meadow to inspect some inquisitive bullocks. And I remember they took Mrs Jelly home in a pony float. She told the driver it was a better 'do' than Mafeking night.

I WAS a child of the era that said I should be seen and not heard. Like an animal in an alien environment I learned the value of stillness, blending with the background, listening keenly and keeping my head down when the conversation of adults grew interesting. It was in such a neutral posture, waiting to be served with a penny stamp in the post office, that in the August of my tenth year I heard startling news. There was to be a village garden party. Now birthday and Christmas parties I knew; they meant food, crackers, balloons, games and a good admixture of ginger pop. But here, as I gathered, was a party in a garden, and mainly for adults. I was convinced there had been a mistake. I couldn't see my father holding a balloon in one hand and bun in the other, and not even my older brothers and sisters in public. Yet the novel rumours persisted and I was perplexed to learn that the party would be held on the lawns of 'The Chestnuts', the home of a gentleman farmer. Perhaps, I mused, these adults would eat at trestle tables on the lawn and have large urns of tea. Yet even this seemed needless discomfort. Why not eat in the village hall?

The mystery deepened when on the day of the party Cecil and I learned that we could go but must pay to enter: something quite outside our experience. A party was a celebration for pleasure, but where was the pleasure if one paid; might just as well buy your own food? However, we concluded, the food was bound to be splendid and might justify spending the entrance money. But how to raise a shilling apiece to enter the banquet? Time was pressing; it was Saturday morning and money must be found by the afternoon. We followed our normal route to wealth and set off rabbiting with Nipper the terrier. We caught two, a buck and a doe, the last in fine condition but alas, clearly still suckling young and showing signs of milk. Still, we reasoned, what the eye doesn't see the heart doesn't grieve. So when we had gutted the doe, we cut back the belly skin on each side to remove the offending nipples. Then off to Mrs Brown, a regular customer; two rabbits for three shillings, a bargain price. We showed her the buck and she fetched the money. We fled before she examined the other.

It was a sultry shirt-sleeve afternoon when Cecil and I parted with a shilling each to pass through the gates of 'The Chestnuts', still with sixpence each to spend should we find good value for money. The terraced lawns had been transformed. One lawn was studded with tents and marquees, and resembled an army encampment. The soldier figures turned out to be bandsmen strutting round an improvised bandstand made by throwing a tarpaulin over a large flat farm trolley. On another terrace women attended to stalls, selling all sorts of pleasing knick-knacks. But these delights must wait. We had paid for a party so off in search of the food. On the furthermost lawns we found games of skill, darts, coconut shies and skittling for a little porker; and beyond that, nothing except fields! Nothing that is, until we glimpsed 'Chopsy' Fowler, squeezing through a hole in the hedge. He was surprised to learn we had paid to enter and, being two years wiser than us, was delighted to expose our folly. There was no free tea, he said; and we had paid a shilling simply to pass through a gate. Retracing our steps we found nothing was free and even the band passed a hat round.

Now normally we wouldn't have paid any attention to Chopsy: nothing but a windbag and a shyster. But Cecil and I were angry and hungry, so we listened to his surefire plan to recoup our loss. In one tent, he said, a man presided over a bucket of water with half-a-crown at the bottom. Drop in a penny that touched this coin and it was yours. Chopsy assured us the odds were eight to one in our favour and if Cecil and I spent fourpence each, success was certain. He regretted he had no money but agreed to advise us in return for twopence of the winnings. The secret, he revealed, was to drop the penny exactly vertical, let it slide down the side of the bucket, and it would slither to the centre. We entered that tent like bandits intent on robbing a bank. I cast first; the penny slid right over the half crown and finished on the opposite side. Cecil's penny waltzed like a floating leaf and missed its target entirely. I repeated my drop, with a result like my first. Cecil was nearer but the bucket seemed big as a pond. 'Drop from lower down,' whispered Chopsy. We did and my coin stood on its edge. Cecil refused to follow and we left the tent in disgust.

I spent my last threepence like a gambler on one last desperate cast. It was one I have never regretted. For three whole minutes I donned headphones and listened to the first radio ever to be heard in our village; it was music from Daventry and I bragged about it for months.

The day was memorable on two more counts. A summer storm broke. Between claps of thunder, the pig-skittling winner was announced. But the piglet had vanished, frightened by the thunder some said. Somehow I wasn't sorry; my loss was much more bearable, for the loss of a good tea seemed quite the equal of that of a little pig. Of course, it may have been accident, but when I met Chopsy two days later, he had just had pork for dinner. Cecil and I fled from the storm to a chestnut tree where two old ladies were standing. We learned our mistake too late. 'You wicked boys,' said a quavering voice, 'you sold me a milky doe. You deserve to be punished.' I could have replied, but hadn't the courage, 'We've been punished already Mrs Brown.'

THE ONLY person in our house who had regular holidays was Mother. She went annually to stay with her sister Kate in Salisbury. Three days before she departed by train, in the interests of economy we began the process of posting food to Auntie. It usually began with the despatch of a chicken in its feathers, brown paper round the head and a label on the legs. By the time Mother arrived, there was cold chicken for tea. Regular daily despatches followed of eggs, ham, hares, rabbits and more chickens. Mother believed in the restorative properties of rest and good food. Aunt Kate, a penniless schoolteacher, was only too happy to follow the same régime.

In one exceptional year, Mother had an extra holiday in early June when lambing and sheepshearing were over and haymaking not yet begun. The weather was so good that Mother wrote to Father, and persuaded him to join her for a few days. His case was packed, and the trap made ready to take him to the station. At that point, a neighbouring farmer arrived. 'Come to see if you can lend me a couple of files,' said he. 'And what might they be for?' enquired Father. 'Well,' came the reply, 'I thought I'd sharpen the grass mower knives, seeing how it's turned warmer. Might make an early start with the hay.' That was enough for Father who reckoned always to be the first man to start grass mowing. 'Unpack my cases. Send

mother a telegram. "Harold coming instead of Father." '
And that's how I took my first real holiday.

Father's sister was married to a farmer who rented a
sizeable and mostly arable farm. He owned two tractors,
several ploughs and a threshing drum. After a particularly
good and early hay harvest Father decided he could
dispense with the services of Cecil and myself and we
could spend the rest of our 'holiday' with Aunt and Uncle.
So one fine day in late July we set off by bicycle after
lunch on the twenty-mile journey into Northamptonshire,
our clothing stowed in rucksacks on the rear carriers.

Despite the heat and the dusty roads, we travelled with
a light heart, for we were venturing into a totally new
world. The very landscape seemed welcoming as we
moved from dark heavy Leicestershire clay to the golden
red soil of the ironstone country. Stone walls replaced
hedges, and fields of ripening wheat, oats, and barley
became more numerous than the lush meadows we were
used to. What we knew of Aunt and Uncle we liked,
although hitherto we had only met them on our own
ground. They were childless but fond of children and we
always remembered their visits for the florins they disbursed on leaving. We savoured, too, their advice,
'Spend it on something nice; you're only young once.'
This bespoke a philosophy of life in direct contrast to the
one we were trained in. Our maxim had been, 'Save for
something useful when you're older.' Cecil and I debated
the contrasting viewpoints as we cycled along towards
what seemed an El Dorado — the very source of the florins
and the pleasing advice to spend. Finally, in anticipation
of wealth to come, we felt justified in buying two penny
ice-cream cornets, but not without some slight sense of
guilt. When Cecil dropped his cornet only half eaten,
we were convinced the gods had frowned on our rash-
ness; until I remembered that we really were hungry,
and Father had often said, 'If you're poor, never let your
stomach know it.'

At length we came to the signpost that said 'Houghton Lodge'. It pointed down a well metalled drive built to take the weight of heavy machinery. We noted with pleasure the well-hung free-swinging gate which we were able to open and pass through without dismounting. No barbed-wire hinges here! All omens were good.

Houghton Lodge was a large square house built of honey-coloured stone. As we viewed it from the drive, it seemed to have grown out of the middle of a barleyfield. The drive itself passed through a field of ripening oats and terminated in the yard surrounding the house. Here two sheep dogs barred the way so I put four fingers in my mouth and whistled shrilly. From under a tractor crawled Uncle and our 'holiday' had really begun. Aunt suggested we would like a light tea after our journey, pending the main meal about seven o'clock. So we sat down in the kitchen to a meal of bread and home-made jam, salad and home-made brawn and a giant sponge cake. To our delight Aunt said the latter needed eating while fresh, so eat it we did. If this was a light tea, I warmed to the prospect of the main meal with only four people to eat it.

Uncle was more academic than Father, having trained and served in the Eastern Telegraph Company before moving into farming for his health's sake. He provided a complete contrast to our father. He was passionately fond of machines and the crops that required them. If he saw grass he wanted to plough it, disc it, sow it, roll it, reap it and plough again. He had a dairy herd and some sheep but simply to provide bread-and-butter money in-between selling his grain crops. To my delight he was never too busy to talk. The sheep could go unshepherded while the intricacies of a threshing machine were explained. While 'footing' the sheep in a pen, the life-cycle of the sheep maggot and the fly that laid the egg were outlined. We discussed the impossibility of perpetual motion and Uncle gave me my first understanding of calculus. Sometimes we would discuss these things while working during the day and pursue them in greater detail during the evening. If there was a mathematical aspect to a problem, so much the better, for Uncle was not only a mathematician but had the happy knack of making all learning a joy and a discovery. Our evenings were passed learning chess and bridge or devouring Arthur Mee's *Children's Encyclopaedia*.

Cecil and I did our share of work as soon as reaping began. We helped with stooking the sheaves like an inverted V, eight to a stook. Nor did we just stook them in lines as they fell, as most farmers did. Each stook was directed to the south-west to obtain maximum effect from sun and wind. Even in the heat of the day, learning had its place. We timed one another to discover how many sheaves we lifted in a minute. In the evening we took a sheaf home to weigh it and worked out how many tons we lifted in a day. At a later stage when some threshed corn was being carried by men up into the granary, Uncle purported to calculate our horsepower by weighing us and then timing how long it took us to run up the granary steps to the loft nine feet above us.

Carting sheaves from stook to stack was one of the toughest jobs I remember: at least for the loaders, Cecil and myself. Men on either side of each wagon pitched the sheaves up, corn heads inwards. The loader must receive them with bare hands, and lock them securely in. The sheaves lay down the wagon in two rows, heads to the centre. A third row was then placed down the centre to bind the others and stop the load slipping. A little respite came as the load grew higher and the men had to lift the sheaves six feet above their own heads. Cecil and I soon learned to estimate the size of our task. Serrated barley whiskers could cut like razors until the hands became well calloused. They crept into socks and shirts and nestled round the neck, waist and ankles like torture rings. Oats were more kindly, except when men pitching them up

gnomes, we headed for the barn, there to leave our spoils till the afternoon. As we entered the stackyard, distinct snores came from the open-fronted barn. Could be a badger, but the sight of smoking wood-ash soon told me differently. Flat on his back in the manger, cushioned in hay and snoring in raucous bursts, lay a tramp. His sodden boots lay drying by the fire's embers and a skip of mushrooms stood close by. Retiring quietly, I planned our attack. With balaclavas completely masking our faces, we stole up and yelled in his ear. The poor fellow woke to see two masked figures armed with hayforks. He leaped from the manger with an agility that belied his ancient looks and fled barefoot without a backward glance. We added his findings to our own but left the skip and his shoes in the middle of the field over which he fled. Next day they were gone.

Rousing the tramp's fire to life, we toasted some bread on the tines of a hayfork and, to add flavour to the ham, shredded onto it the pale pink fins of some of our tenderest mushrooms. Later that day, on the way home, we called on 'The Mushroom Man'. He came regularly throughout the season to a hut which he hired on the village outskirts. He bought mushrooms from all and sundry and resold to the ketchup factories in the town. The condition of the mushrooms didn't matter. He accepted the black and maggoty mulch in the bottom of our baskets as readily as the beautiful chocolate-finned dewfresh platers on top of our loads, and he paid well. Most of our earnings went to Mother but we always had a penny or two to spend at the post office shop. Naturally, too, we always had plenty of fried mushrooms for breakfast.

Pocket money, in the sense of something for nothing, was unknown in our household. It had to be earned from some external source. That is to say, work for any member of the family was regarded as a duty. In any case, payment for this sort of work would simply be an internal transfer of money, bringing no net gain to the family, and even a loss if it was spent. When we did earn money from mush-rooming or the like, we were sometimes allowed to keep a portion, if it was spent on something that could be described by Mother as 'sensible'; this usually meant some article of clothing or something for the bicycle, like a tyre or a pump.

Our favourite way to quick cash in the winter was through rabbiting at which we became experts. Our chief ally was our terrier called Nipper who could not have been more aptly named. No dog knew more about self-control, and the use of surprise against an enemy. The technique which Nipper really taught himself was simple. Once he had scented a rabbit in the hedge, instead of rushing after it like other dogs, he moved away downwind and sat stock still, either in the centre of the hedge or the bottom of the ditch. He left us to create the noise and hullaballoo, to beat the hedge and drive the quarry down the hedge straight into his waiting jaws. We never inflicted needless pain on any animal, for we had a deep respect for wildlife.

By the age of fourteen, I was allowed to use a twelve-bore shotgun against rabbits provided there were only two of us, and we stayed close together. Too many people, Father said, had been shot through hedges. Perhaps it was just as well I could shoot, for about this time we lost Nipper. Daily when we drove to the main farm, he trotted along with us. While we worked in the fields, he hunted for rabbits. On the outskirts of the village lived the District Nurse, and as we passed her cottage each morning, she took to giving Nipper a snack, usually meat scraps, for she lived alone. At first he only paused briefly, gobbled his titbits, and soon caught up with us. But as he grew older, and the delights of the chase waned, his delays became longer, till one day he abandoned us com-pletely. From that day forward, Nipper adopted the nurse and lived in some luxury. But daily as we passed his new home, he stood on a box provided by his mistress and barked furiously over the hedge as if to say, 'I don't care for you now; keep away.' He never returned to the farm and lived to the age of fifteen. The process of his adoption was of course amicable, and he was good company for his new owner. She, alas, was killed while visiting a patient on her bicycle. She was found unconscious at the bottom of a steep hill, where the road ran through open fields. The only clue to the tragedy was sheep's wool in the spokes of her front wheel. Nipper had died a few days previously.

I T WAS April 23rd, 1922: my birthday and I was going to visit my grandparents. There was promise of reward on both counts. The previous day, Friday, in school, Miss Banner called the register and paused — 'Harold George Cramp, you are ten tomorrow, and may sit on the back row on Monday.' I was stirred by the prospect of new-found delights attaching to my new status: walking round the class filling inkwells while others sat with arms folded; shaking the blackboard duster outside and listening to the drone of infant voices; shovelling coke into the tortoise stove and watching the belch of blue flame. Real power awaited me. But sweetest privilege of all was to be dismissed first at break. No more stampede to the toilets where the pressure to enter defeated the efforts to emerge. And first at the drinking-water bucket with its iron cup, which each successive drinker must hastily rescue by plunging his arm into the water, up to the elbow.

Having savoured the joys of Monday to come, my thoughts returned to Saturday present. Who, over breakfast, would remember my birthday? For a time no one did. Then my eldest brother glanced at the daily paper and remarked, 'Bless me, it's Saint George's Day, and Harold's birthday. Well done lad! A few more Christmas puddings and you'll be really useful at harvest time.'

There was mumbled support for this sentiment from one or two others. Then, as if assessing a show beast, Father eyed me and said, 'Must be well over five feet now. Growing into real strength. Mind you, height can be overdone. Anything over five feet ten is waste.' For a moment I was worried. I had often seen adverts which promised, for a fee, to increase your height, but none to slow growth down. Besides, I could never afford it, so dismissed the idea.

My brother and I rushed through the Saturday jobs. We flung the hens' corn with abandon, not bothering to seek dry ground; hurled broody hens from their nest-boxes, smashing eggs in so doing; instead of cleaning out the henhut, disguised the muck with new straw. Then a quick change of clothes and we headed for Shangton and our grandparents, and freedom too. By opening a field gate and clapping it hard shut we roused every thrush and blackbird nearby, and soon located the nests. We admired the azure blue of the thrushes' eggs, placed some in a blackbird's nest and swore to follow the outcome. But we never did. We shook pigeons' eggs from their precarious platforms in hawthorn bushes and watched a green woodpecker hammering for beetles. We encountered the roadman, a notorious poacher. He drifted to the opposite side of the road as we approached, but he stank of rabbits as we passed him. He carried a ferret in his trouser pocket, sent it down drainpipes which ran under the road, and netted the emerging quarry.

Soon we branched from the main highway down a muddy lane to Shangton, a sad little hamlet which died with the field enclosures. Once a majestic elm avenue had lined our route. Now dead trees outnumbered the living. Here and there half-dead limbs drooped to earth from splintered trunks, still drawing sap briefly, reluctant to die while the parent still lived. Fractured stumps, barkless and white, stood like monuments to some aborted plan of Nature, while thrusting through rank grasses were giant puffballs and blood-red toadstools, obscenely beautiful ornaments of corruption. It oppressed us and we kicked out wildly at colonies of poisonous brown fungi, only to see them turn red under our assaults as if blushing at their own deception.

The Shangton hamlet crouched in a bowl between two hills. Even in springtime the birdsong seemed muffled by damp air, the wet earth and the tree-clad slopes. Mounds topped by nettle and elder marked the last homes of a forgotten peasantry. Only in the churchyard the Hackneys and Hills proclaimed how once they made the valley fertile. There were few to disturb their peace now. A bachelor farmer survived at the Hall, with an ancient house-keeper whom few had seen. The Parson and his wife were entombed in a thirty-room rectory, while my grand-parents lived quietly in their cottage.

The lane by which we descended arrived at the centre of the hamlet, turned sharply and climbed back to the main road, as if anxious not to be lost. Winter's springs still oozed from the banks, and cows seeking a soft footing had so trodden out the verges that the metalled road was barely visible. We drew level with the church and decided to enter. It conveyed neither the dignity of age without, nor the beauty of holiness within; and was damp and ruinous. Inside the nave a few peasants had been pro-moted, for their headstones had been placed round the walls to hide the slimy suppurations from decaying stonework. Their marble-faced betters looked coldly down.

We were glad to escape back to the churchyard where a sharp tapping gave semblance of life. This was traced to a thrush smashing a snail shell on a tombstone engraved 'In Everlasting Memory' of some ancient who had died 'aged 84 years' but whose name was now etched in slow devouring moss.

With our feet under Grandma's lunch table we told Grandpa about the thrush and asked what would become of the church, for he always had time to answer our questions. 'Material things are immaterial,' he explained. Churches were just stones really and it didn't matter whether you were born in a manger or buried in an orange box (and he had seen both). It was people who mattered and making the best of even a bad job. As for the thrushes, they would still be hammering snails in a thousand years. Only man could rise to a fuller state of life in this world and the next.

After lunch we explored the barns, ground the cattle cake, groomed the pony and oiled his harness. Only once did our zeal bring us to the verge of trouble. In the bottom of a barrel we found twelve eggs — obviously a hen 'laying away' — and hastened to tell Grandpa. His answer abashed us but he took us into his secret. Grandma liked a regular egg supply so he satisfied her by the magic of averages, keeping a reserve in his barrel. Granny was kept happy and her income from egg sales suffered little variation.

Grandma's birthday tea included my favourites — red jelly in abundance, sandwich cake with bramble jelly, and her home-made lemon curd and cream cheese. Then after tea a special look at the family Bible with the births of all nine of us listed. The name of my eldest brother headed the list inside the front cover: Robert Raymond Kingston Cramp. Pride showed in every stroke of the copperplate writing. The name of my eldest sister, Muriel Kate, appeared with equal dignity. But from then on the entries lacked the same quality, as if the main task of perpetuating the family had been achieved, and succeeding names had the status of mere reserves. Times of birth ceased to appear as the list lengthened, and number six was wedged in at the bottom of the cover as if surely that was the last. To accommodate the next three, myself and Cecil included, the fly leaf had been brought into use and I just had time to read that after the last name someone had written 'God help Ethel' which I knew referred to Mother. Cecil went quiet when Granny observed that, of all nine children, only he had just one Christian name. He seemed further upset by the fact that Grandma's dentures caused her to whistle whenever she spoke his name.

Churchyard and Church

IN LANGTON death figured as one of the healthy topics of conversation. Along with births, christenings and marriages, it vied with the weather for interest. Nor had death morbid overtones. For most villagers, survival here was a much more pressing concern than worry about the hereafter; death was usually regarded as 'a happy release' or a satisfactory end to 'a good innings'. Either way there was usually a family celebration, when the dead man's life was freely discussed, including his frailties. As for his present whereabouts, 'He'll be better off where he is.' When manual labour dominated men's lives it was easy to regard death as a long sleep. 'He rests from his labours' was a satisfying thought in a funeral service or on a headstone.

Some neighbouring villages had cemeteries, remote from the village scene; sad awkward islands carved out of good meadow land. Here in revenge, the grass sought to get the better of white hygienic headstones, marble chippings and jam jars full of dead flowers. 'Take your rubbish to the far corner', spelled a notice in one cemetery. Could this apply to the dead likewise, hidden away in a field? Not if you came from Langton. We were too proud to hide our dead. Church and churchyard lay at the heart of the village. Only iron rails halfway up the main street separated the dead from the living. A low brick wall marked the other three sides of the churchyard. One wall backed on to a cottage garden. Here on Mondays Mrs Bolton hung her washing to dry. The rest of the week her family of five, all under eight, used the wall for acrobatic tricks. Sometimes they earned an honest penny by showing enquiring strangers round the church. By adding a little fiction to fact, they found they could sometimes earn tuppence. Hence we acquired ghosts, hidden vaults and the highest steeple in the Midlands.

Thus did the living and the dead dwell happily together. The doings of the latter were good for many a tale over a pint in the Crown Inn opposite the church. Indeed the quickest way for a stranger to investigate our ancestry was to 'stand treat' to the older labourers and listen. Then, for instance, he might learn of the skill of the farmer Matthias Swingler who could fire a marble from a catapult and kill a rabbit at twenty paces. Or the tale of John Hill, who slipped off steps when hanging half a pig from a beam in the larder. The pig fell to the floor while John was left hanging with a hook through his wrist till his wife found him an hour later. Her first question when entering the larder was, 'Whatever's happened to the pig?' Then there was Dick Mills the carrier, whose grave never lacked flowers whatever the season. It was said that the women could pay him in cash or in bed. His offspring marked the route of his carrier's cart and were all distinguished by a good Roman nose which was Dick's outstanding feature. Some very old men would relate the story of Gibby, a former roadman. The left hand that he lost in a chaff cutter was replaced by a steel hook screwed into a cork pad on the stump of his wrist. He grasped brush or shovel with the right hand while the handle of the tool slid freely in the hook. All went well till walking home in a thunderstorm. The lightning struck his hook and killed him. One interesting story concerned two farming brothers who sold several fields and kept the money in a wooden box under the bull's manger. Their expectation of retirement with plenty was marred when they found that rats had eaten their way through several thousand pounds.

The old folks in the village represented our roots. Like ancient oak trees they gave a comfortable sense of permanence. They represented survival, sometimes it seemed against all the odds. If these ancients were still telling life's story, what unlimited hopes and possibilities, I thought, still awaited me. When I gazed at the lined parchment of old Collins's face, I knew what eternity was. When he told me of his childhood days they seemed primaeval times and a million years ago. If one day he should no longer look over his gate, I thought, he would still be around, albeit invisible. I could never think of death as an end of things; that would be such a waste.

Collins was stooped, nay bowed, from years of toil, first as a ploughman, later as a gardener. When the weather was fine, especially in the evening when there were folks to talk to, he would lean, or rather hang, over his front gate. So bent was his back, it was difficult for him to look up. So he mainly looked sideways up and down our one main street; but sometimes he gazed down at the earth at the foot of his gate. And it was in this position that neighbours found him. They'd never have known anything was wrong except that his clay pipe lay on the path in front of his gate, broken but still smouldering.

It was not unusual for men especially to die at their work. Take old Burrell the hedgecutter. One winter afternoon he just failed to return at his usual time. His wife who went in search found him dead, slumped on the bank of the ditch he was working in, and still grasping his bill-hook. Some said it should have been buried with him, but his son was a hedgecutter too and thought it too fine a thing to waste.

Some deaths were more tragic. The farming slump in the Twenties took its toll. Two farmers whom I knew were found shot — accidentally was the Coroner's verdict, but we who knew the fields empty of stock, the hedges uncut, the houses unpainted, the children brought back from private schools prematurely, had other thoughts. These were proud men who provided work and livelihood for half a dozen labouring families. They felt that they had let the community down and death was their protest at a fate worse than death.

Some deaths among farmworkers had rather unusual causes. There was old Siddons and his son who both died of anthrax after burying a bullock which died of the same disease; Mason who was dragged into a power-driven chaff-cutter; Vendy who was gored by a bull when returning home across fields from his allotment; Peterson who stabbed his foot with a muck-fork and died of lockjaw.

Saddest of all were those who died of the dreaded consumption, as tuberculosis was then often called. There were few effective government regulations about milking herds in the Twenties. Bovine tuberculosis was widespread and much milk was infected. When a cow started to 'go off' and the farmer suspected the worst, he simply got rid of it, but some other unfortunate farmer probably bought it and spread the infection. When the veterinary surgeon came round to farms on his government-sponsored inspections, some farmers drove suspect animals to remote parts of the farm until the inspection was over. Milk was milk, they said; they drank it with no harm done so why bother with newfangled ideas. They were not prepared to risk their livelihood by having several animals sent to the knackerman. No doubt many people inherited or developed immunity to tuberculosis, and I never knew of a mature adult being infected. But during my adolescence several of my contemporaries were striken with consumption and wasted away. One youth tried to ward off the evil day by living in a specially designed wooden hut in the garden, to obtain the maximum fresh air. Death was but briefly delayed.

I became aware of one small facet of attending to the dead when I met the undertaker one day coming from the house of one Tailby. He had a tape measure in his hand. 'Just been to measure Charlie,' he said. 'Five foot ten he is. Not bad for a man of eighty.' Now what was the point of measuring Charlie, I wondered. It seemed such an odd thing to do. Was he going to buy a new suit? And if so, why couldn't his wife do it? Zach must have noticed my puzzled look for he continued, 'Died peacefully in his sleep last night. Most folk lose an inch in height for every five years over sixty. But not Charlie; he kept fit by spudding thistles.' This last information I knew well. Charlie never retired fully but did thistling on a piecework basis. I never knew him without a long white beard. He looked patriarchal and reminded me of the picture of Abraham in the Infants' Department at School. He was buried in a plain deal coffin, as were most of the poorer folk; not for them polished oak, heavy with brass ornament.

Evidence of the village social structure was to be seen in the churchyard amongst the dead as clearly as in the village amongst the living. Betwixt the main street and the church entrance tombstones were few and splendid. Here lay the mighty, even in death asserting their greatness. Some had chains surrounding their family plot. Yet other tombs bore family emblems lest during their lives you had failed to recognise the merits of the deceased. Still it all impressed visitors and made us feel quite important.

At the back of the church and clustered closely round it came the next social layer; the yeomen like ourselves. It was almost as if they sought security in proximity to the church, or wanted to preserve their group economic identity even in death. The richer ones were buried side by side; but most of the yeomen, with a rare sense of economy, were buried in depth, husband and wife one above the other, frugal to the last. They lay 'in certain hope of resurrection' or otherwise protesting their faith. In the calmer corners of the churchyard, away from the fretful words engraved on marble and stone, a ripple of low green mounds marked the graves of ordinary folk. These could not afford to buy their graves in advance and so were tucked in wherever there was space. Their lasting memorial lay in the ridge and furrow of meadows beyond the churchyard wall. If they had hopes of a heaven, I liked to think they encompassed some of the simple joys of life. Such no doubt were also the hopes of the nameless yeoman whose broken slate headstone asked:

> Tell me friend, in accents low
> Does still the woodbine sweetly blow?

I HAVE KNOWN wet 'back-ends' of the year when harvest festivals mocked the name; hay still in cob, bleached to a dirty white, hanging lank like an old man's hair; corn sheaves still in stook in October and sprouting in the head. But the Parson, whose gaitered feet had never trodden a field, sang *Harvest Home* just the same, because his diary said he must. For his pains he spoke to a congregation of aged spinsters, ladies with autumn fashions to parade, children under duress and folk who had walked from neighbouring villages and wanted a dry haven till the pubs opened. Most villagers, with surer instinct than the Parson, preferred Nature's calendar, and some semblance of harvest truly home. They needed something to sing about. When the bounty of field and hedgerow, garden and allotment was garnered in a good season, they swarmed into church with pagan fervour, certain that God was a countryman who had given special attention to Langton. They were equally certain that God had only a passing interest in machines and factories, and God's enemy the Devil largely inhabited the towns. Towns were all right in their way and there were bargains to be had in the Saturday market. But it was a tinsel and glitter world, and those who paid a visit were usually glad to get home. They set out to town with warnings to 'watch your purse'. They returned to sceptical queries of, 'What rubbish have you bought?'

Over the years, the Parson learnt some sense. The harvest festival sermon was no longer heavy with learning and all those difficult-to-understand things about sin and repentance. It was about a God of Nature who saw to it that we had three meals a day. The baker usually got a mention since that was the cue for a reference to yeast and the uplifting power of a little goodness. Besides, on the altar were his long plaited loaves such as he never baked in the normal way of things.

Days before the harvest service, moss by the sackful was plundered from local spinneys. Among village women there had grown a tradition that moss, earthy and damp, must be the basis of most festival displays. It lay through the church like a green rash, on pulpit and font, altar rails and window ledges. It fouled the Parson's sermon notes, dropped on the organ keys, dripped from the candelabra. Combined with the scent of flowers it produced a death-in-life aroma that said corruption lurked where beauty dwelt.

Yet out of the moss grew a banquet of food and flowers. Girding the font were corn sheaves from the manor, specially selected of course, thistle-free and bound with corn stems, not binder twine. Nestling by the pulpit was a hen's nest of moss containing twelve matching brown eggs, the likes of which had never been seen in a henroost at any one time. The lectern eagle looked slightly silly with a Bible on its back, moss on its legs and black grapes draped round its neck.

A walk round the aisles was like a stroll through a horticultural show and a botanical garden combined. Every neo-Gothic column had its spiralling ivy, reaching down to the plinth and trailing so freely it threatened to trap the unwary. Every windowsill had such an avalanche of produce, that to sit beneath it was an act of faith. The scent of end-season roses fought bravely against the pungent bouquet from wild flowers and tired grasses, gathered by ambitious children to out-do their moss-ridden parents.

The few regular church-goers sat in their usual seats, hogging the kneelers and such Ancient and Moderns as had survived intact the assaults of mice, bats and beetles. These faithful arrived early to make sure they were not crowded out by the casuals and the ungodly. The latter groups tended to sit in the pew adjacent to the window which held the produce they had donated, as if anxious that the Almighty and everyone else should know. There were whispered comments during every hymn and chant. 'Has old Smith really grown those carrots?' 'Does that marrow look like the one lost from the allotments a week ago?' 'Are leeks that size really fit to eat?' 'What's going to happen to all the stuff afterwards? Does the Parson have it or the Salvation Army?'

The first lesson from the Old Testament was read by the Lord of the Manor. Tweedily clad, but in finer check than on week-days, he strode to the lectern, face purple as the grapes round the eagle's neck. He was not a good reader, and hated his task, fortified though he was by liquor beforehand. But his titular post of Vicar's Warden demanded this annual appearance, and his arrogant wife insisted. After the 'Here beginneth' no verb or full stop came to rescue the meaning, though the voice flung about from falsetto to basso profundo in an effort to find one.

The Parson droned through his sermon, only interrupted twice by children wailing to be allowed to answer the call of Nature, which was duly done behind headstones in the churchyard. There were five hymns during which the skeletal choir was quite drowned, as the voices of the habitués of the 'middle pub' contended with those from the 'top pub'. Once the organ seemed to lose its way, though some said afterwards it was the fault of the organ blower, who, over-excited by the occasion, had paused in his pumping to relieve himself in the tin he kept specially in the blower's den. When it came to 'We plough the fields and scatter', whole pews turned round to look at Joe Vendy who had won the previous season's ploughing competition and Joe, to be suitably modest, also turned round and looked into space.

The collection during the final hymn became a major event. Separate wardens were needed for all three aisles.

Those people sitting in the rear pews studied the beige-covered silver collection plates for a sight of the crisp new notes and mint silver coins traditionally given by the richer folk towards the front. But as the wardens moved down the church, pretending not to notice who was giving what, mounds of copper coin gradually submerged all else. A few half pence slipped from the hands of over-anxious children. Some fell through the floor gratings on to the oil stoves below. But any wailing at this misfortune was well drowned by the final stanzas of 'Come ye thankful people, come'. In any case, everybody knew that Ted Medowes, Verger and church cleaner, would be the beneficiary and he, being widowed, could do with every penny.

After the Parson had chanted the blessing, the congregation as usual made as if to go home, but were quite confounded by the choir, who suddenly rose and broke into a seven-fold Amen on which no one else had bargained. There was muttered appreciation at this innovation and one or two people were so excited they clapped. Everybody felt better for the experience. While women and children wandered round the churchyard to admire the scrollwork in the slate headstones and sometimes identify their ancestors, the men adjourned to the Crown Inn and the Bull's Head, to celebrate harvest home in extra pints of mild and bitter, and praise the men who grew the hops.

Feeling the Draught

FATHER'S ultimate purposes in life seem to have been enshrined in rare bits of wisdom he occasionally pronounced, especially at mealtimes. One maxim was, 'Work and save till you can live like a gentleman and eat from the back end of a bullock.' Sirloin was the ultimate food for Father, and to his credit we were rarely short of good meat, though, as a growing boy, I felt hungry more often than I felt satisfied. Father's sayings stirred my imagination and I sometimes dreamed that we would one day live in a vast baronial hall, and dine off a great roast ox, such as I had seen pictured in my history books. And there would be meat left over; enough even for the dogs.

Up to the age of eleven, my world seemed solid and reassuring. The unhurried farm routine over which Father presided was like a warm cocoon. Life seemed happy and predictable, and I was conscious that even the small tasks I performed added something to the general harmony. With the conservatism of the very young I loved to find everything in its accustomed place: new bread in the wire safe, left by the baker on Wednesday and Saturday; the tea laid ready when I peered through the kitchen window, and the cat on the hearth. Familiar noises too were comforting: the sound of the dog's tail threshing the sides of his kennel as he recognised my footsteps, but was too idle to stir himself and come out; the noise of sparrows quarrelling for living space in the ivy on the housefront; and the shrill call of a bantam cock kept by a near neighbour. When I had been in the fields all day, even the smell of the home farmyard seemed a satisfying cloak. I felt sorry for children of small families who had to sleep in a bedroom all by themselves or play in the village street because they had no yards and fields.

But this cosy world was not to last, and as I matured into my teens, I became increasingly aware that our family destiny might not be entirely in our own hands; that if the price of meat, milk and wool was low, there was little we could do about it except cut expenses and work harder. From private conversations between Father and Mother that I sometimes overheard, it was clear that we were not immune to disaster. Father said increasingly openly after a bad hay harvest in 1925 that any slackening of effort, any unforeseen major expenditure, any more prolonged adverse weather, any unfortunate deaths in flocks or herds and we should all 'feel the draught'. Cases were cited of farmers who had been forced to sell up and become mere labourers, or at best, farm bailiffs. My sensitive nature soon turned possibility into certainty and for a time I lived in fear of certain special disasters, foremost being foot-and-mouth disease. As I have said, our farm lay in two portions, one at the back of the house and the main part a mile away, at Shangton, where my paternal grandparents lived on a smallholding. If ever, when shepherding, we found signs of the disease on the Shangton farm we were told never to return to the home farm, in case contagion was brought to the dairy herd. Instead, we must report to Grandfather, who would check our suspicions. As a result, the sight of a bullock that limped or appeared to slobber, saw me running in terror half a mile to fetch Grandfather. His philosophical approach to life always comforted me, and the worst never came to pass.

The second pestilence that did sometimes strike was contagious abortion, or 'slip-calf' disease in the cows. This was a positive threat to our monthly lifeline, the milk cheque. The disease was one of the few problems which really upset Father. Bacterial infection could not be grasped, responded to no inherited skills or hard work, and gave no warning of its coming. The best we could do was to 'sprayclean' the cowsheds more frequently, lime-wash the walls again and again, and spray gallons of disinfectant in the infected area.

Times must have been bad when in 1925 Father regarded even a light 'fall' of lambs as a serious body-blow; less lambs, less sheep, less wool was the reasoning. When some local farmers lost sheep at lambing time, they would not bother to hand-rear the lambs or 'hang them on' to other mothers. But Father knew every such-minded farmer, and sent us boys scouring the district for spare lambs. We could always, with patience, make a ewe with a single lamb adopt a second, or keep a reserve pool of 'cades', or hand-fed orphan lambs. As Father never tired of telling us, 'Little lambs become big sheep, come mint sauce time.'

An air of crisis always seemed to descend on the family at tithe-paying time, when 'Queen Anne's Bounty' as it was called had to be rendered to the Church Commissioners. Since we owned our farm, Father regarded tithes as an unjust rent exacted by the Church, the more so as most neighbouring farmers were free of this imposition. Father grumbled, 'If it weren't for the tithes, I'd be sure of having a fair year,' but with the clear implication that there were now doubts about our solvency.

A hazard the whole family feared was fire. Our farm-house was old and all ceilings were supported by revealed oak beams. Chimneys frequently caught fire in winter-time. No matter how well swept, soot always collected on concealed ledges, till finally it caught fire and burnt itself out. How near to disaster we could come was revealed one autumn, when four of us boys, sleeping in a large bed-room, complained that we were too hot at night. Father was immediately curious, went to the bedroom and felt the floor. From the chimney stack to some four feet out into the room, it was distinctly hot. Mr Busby the carpenter was immediately sent for, carpets lifted and floorboards removed. The cause was quickly visible. One oak beam terminated inside the chimney. Removal of a few bricks showed that nothing had protected the end of the beam except a slate nailed on. Only the nail and a slate fragment remained. A spark had ignited the end grain of the centuries-old oak, which now glowed like charcoal. Over the weeks the burning had moved slowly along the beam. Such gases as were given off must have been drawn back into the chimney, for we smelt nothing. Fortunately the beam was so massive as to need no renewing.

Apart from the house, haystacks standing side by side in the home farmyard were most vulnerable to fire. Stacks on the farm were sited well away from roads. In the home yard where there could be over a hundred tons of hay, no one was allowed to smoke. Since none of the family smoked, the rule applied to workmen and visitors. On Guy Fawkes night we boys patrolled the hayricks looking and listening in case glowing rocket sticks fell in the hay. Not for us the frivolity of 'burning money' as Father said.

The frequent air of crisis in the family affected me much, particularly when going to bed after hearing a discussion on farm problems. Till the age of twelve I had horrific nightmares. But apart from giving me Carr's Fever Powders when I woke screaming, no one bothered to wonder if my imagination was fevered with good cause.

A corollary of Father's repeated forecasts of disaster was his theory that one must have 'reserves'. When one farmer shot himself in the early Twenties, Father's wisdom seemed proven. So there were reserves everywhere. First and foremost on the farm they took the form of stacks of hay. We made hay on half the farm every year. Every field had at least one hayrick, some had two or three. There was not only enough hay to feed our own stock, but some to sell and some in reserve in case of a dry summer later on. This last could be instantly realised in cash by sale to hunting stables or forage merchants. Every haystack was painstakingly thatched. 'Who would

be so silly as to leave the lid off a bucket of sovereigns?'
Father would muse. Where we saw only hay, Father saw
a pound sign writ large. He had only to stride out the
length and breadth of a haystack and glance at the height
to tell how many tons it contained. He would estimate the
quality of the hay by circling the stack, pushing his arm
deep into the sides and withdrawing samples. He would
examine the herbage, sniff it, and straightaway tell the
worth of the hayrick.

The second reserve was hand-reared calves. Wherever
there was space in the farmyard, there was a calf. I have
known a horse in one half of a stable and three calves in
the other half. Mother swore Father would have one in
the kitchen if she'd allow it. For half an hour before
feeding time every day, they bawled their heads off.
Whenever Mother complained that she received much of
the benefit through the kitchen window, Father would
reply, 'The louder the anthem the bigger the choir,' or,
'Where there's noise there's numbers.' Secretly Mother
was in agreement for wasn't the cackling of a laying hen
just as sweet music to her? Quiet farmyards, we all knew,
are nobody's friend.

Some calves were reared in old pigsties; these were
only cleaned out once a year, but fresh straw bedding was
added several times weekly. As it decomposed with the
dung, it generated warmth and formed a sort of central
heating which suited the calves. When the time came for
cleaning out these particular sties in the spring, the muck
had grown so high that the calves had a job to get out of
the doorway into the small exercise area. They had usually
scuffed all the hair from their backs in executing this daily
manoeuvre.

Reserves in the house were so immense that we could
have withstood a siege. In the winter we slaughtered three
pigs, so year-long the kitchen walls were lined with hams
and whole flitches of bacon on which the salt glistened
hard and white. Bacon was cut daily as required, so at a

glance one could see how this particular asset was eking out. Quite literally we ate our way through to the kitchen walls. When, by the end of October, all bacon and hams had been consumed, the kitchen looked strangely naked though a good deal larger. There is no doubt that the large stocks of home-produced and preserved food found in the houses of all the yeomen I knew, gave them a sense of independence, well-being and pride, as well as making for a good table and good health.

Apples from our large orchard were stored in the attics. Northing Greens would keep there until apples came again. We had boiled apple puddings and apple pies several times every week. Autumn was the great storage time. Mother pickled onions, cabbage, and walnuts, made chutney in large stone jars, and also mushroom ketchup. Jam was made in quantities that required the use of the giant washday 'copper'. It held ten gallons. We jammed apples, blackberries, blackcurrants, damsons and raspberries, using preserving sugar that came in half-hundredweight bags. The pantry shelves groaned with jars and where they sagged in the middle, they were strapped to ceiling beams by iron brackets, inserted by some former thrifty yeoman and still bearing the hammer marks of some local smith.

Father's one concession to agriculture was to plough a narrow strip in an allotment to grow enough potatoes and turnips for a year. These were clamped at home, and drawn as required.

Coal featured importantly in the storage process. It was ordered by the ten-ton railway truck every autumn, and hauled some two and a half miles from the railway station. When stacked in giant lumps, this 'Derbyshire Bright' half-filled the back kitchen from floor to ceiling, and lasted a whole year. It was of course eked out with logs of wood. No vehicle ever returned home from the main farm without bits of old fencing posts, rotten rails, broken limbs from hedgerow trees (mostly ash), and the thicker limbs from some very old hedges which had to be cut to make them stockproof.

Father satisfied part of his needs and 'avoided loss' by using a barter system. Thus, we rarely paid a bread or flour bill. Instead the cost was offset by supplying the baker's horses with fodder and providing him with one or two sheep to help graze his paddock. Our household flour was stacked on a wooden platform in a corner of the kitchen. A large lump of suet always nestled in the top of the sack to keep it fresh.

Doctor's bills were paid on the same barter basis. We supplied him with fodder for the horse that pulled his gig and also grazed his spare horse. To obtain medicines, one of the family was sent with a note describing the symptoms and Dr Collington prescribed accordingly. He was only asked to come in real emergencies. Even the blacksmith's bill was partly offset by hauling his iron bars from railway station to smithy. By such 'scheming and skimping' we weathered the hard times.

Life Springs a Trap

UP TO THE AGE of eleven, life seemed firmly within my grasp. My environment was known and safe. People, buildings, animals, fields, I knew them all. I could tell you how often old York trimmed his beard, when the next village baby was due, how far Ted Ward could spit on a still day, what had given Mapley a double hernia, why May Briggs had been jilted, and who was suspected of milking cows at dead of night in the field, to provide nourishment for a half-starved family. Did you wish to see the burrow of a rabbit, the grassy tunnel of a field mouse, the skeleton of a crow, the feathers of a guinea fowl, the nest of a peewit, I could take you directly. I knew the origin of every bark, bellow, howl, rumble and screech that came to my ears. The state of village health I knew well; who had ringworm, nits in the hair, boils on the bottom, ulcers on the leg or congestion in the lungs. Climbable trees, jumpable streams, gaps in hedges, shelter in hollow trees, ponds so deep they rarely froze, were all part of my repertoire. Most days my heart found time and reason to sing and the village was rich in echoes.

It was 1924 when life sprang its first trap on me. One blustery March day that year I was rollicking along to school with my friends. It was the sort of wind that whips off a boy's hat and parts his hair in the wrong places. It ballooned up our short trousers and thundered in our ears. We teased the girls who spun like tops as they fought with skirts that whipped over their heads. They enjoyed the wind's mischief but gave us shrill orders to walk on ahead. I remember these things, for that same March wind blew me a change of fortune that lasted for the rest of my days.

To be called to the front of the class by the Headmaster

was a challenge to the nerves. His poker face and dry humour always left the issue uncertain. Would there be a pat on the shoulder or a box on the ears, a question about work or a forgotten misdemeanour? Even innocent boys said silent prayers and guilty ones had been known to extend a hand before the cane was even produced. So when four names were called including mine, we gathered weak-kneed round the Headmaster's desk, so close I could see the hairs in his nostrils and some shaving soap in his ear.

The four of us learned, 'Opinion is that you have some brains and it's time we gave them an airing. I've decided to enter you for Grammar School entrance scholarship in a month's time.' The Head dwelt for a moment on the horrors of failure, sucked air through his teeth and seemed for a moment to glance at his cane. Then he suddenly smiled and barked, 'Well done,' as though we had already passed the exam.

For four long weeks we were pampered with attention and force-fed with knowledge. Arithmetic was always the main course of the day before our brains grew addled. The last 'amen' of Assembly had hardly sounded before we were into a diet of rods and chains, pennyweights and farthings, and all those subtleties bequeathed by our Anglo-Saxon forebears. We paid men for hedging at ten shillings a chain, grocers for essence at three farthings a gill, farmers for corn at four pounds a quarter.

I learned the wizardries of quick-method mental arithmetic. I could gaze into space, or focus on a dirty window pane, and mentally purchase 999 clothes pegs at a halfpenny each or a gross of jampot covers at a penny for twelve. Between break and lunchtime I could build you an essay on the humblest of everyday themes, rolling a giant snow ball from a small and innocent core. We had likely essays already handmade on Springtime, The Wembley Exhibition, The Advantages of Motorcars, The British Empire, or Imagine you are a penny and tell your life

story. We could fill a page of foolscap in forty-five minutes
and lard it with predigested vocabulary. I could slot a
'fascinating', an 'unforgettable' or a 'marvellous' into any
essay you cared to name. And never a blot on the whole
page, being trained to draw my pen nib over the edge of
the inkwell like a bird wiping its beak on a gutter. Snacks
of History, Geography, General Knowledge and Daily
News filled our afternoons but this was only lightweight
stuff to show in oral interview how worldly-wise an eleven
year old can be.

The exam was set for a Saturday. I was wakened early
and dressed as for Sundays to impress the oral examiner.
I was given one cup of tea only, otherwise 'You'll be in
and out of the toilet like a two year old.' Finally, I was
given tuppence to signify the importance of the occasion
— 'and make sure you earn it.' I spent it on sherbet at the
post office shop and felt quite sick by the time I reached
school. But the day went well. The exam paper sparkled
with old friends: the Wembley Exhibition, grocer's
bills, taps filling baths, and converting pounds into
farthings. I returned home in triumph only to be casti-
gated over the sherbet, for Mother had called on the
shop and learned of my wanton spending.

Some four weeks later, on April the first, 'Master
Harold Cramp' received his exam result. I had won a
Grammar School place; and the honour of cycling five and
a half miles to school each day including Saturday morning; the pleasure of doing games on Saturday afternoon if
required, and two hours' homework each evening. I was
delivered into an alien system on the September day I
cycled off for the first time.

New boys like myself were bundled into the Domestic
Science room (no chairs of course) there to wait like a
dangerous species, while the rest of the school sang 'Lord
receive us with thy blessing'. Assembly over, older boys
looked at us through a glass screen and threatened us with
an early death; one of our number who sought the toilets

was shown into the girls' place. My breakfast was already
two and a half hours away when the Headmaster entered
our room, picking his nose. My marching orders were,
'Shell form, four-year course to Matric, room 4, and get a
move on.' Nothing in my previous life seemed to have
relevance any more, but I had already learned one thing.
Whatever the school might teach me, I could teach them a
thing or two.

My form master was a little squirt of a man who wore
double-thick soles to give himself a lift. His pince-nez
glasses and bony nose put me in mind of a predatory
bird. To ensure class control he harassed us daily with
meaningless disciplines and for the first time in my life I
hated a man. Most of the school's pupils came from the
town. To me they appeared prissily dressed, slick, self-
satisfied and prettily mannered. The boys arrived with
excessively polished shoes, well creased trousers, solid
leather satchels and looking every inch like a bunch of
little Lord Fauntleroys. The gymslipped girls looked
prim, confident and leggy with black stockings that went
up and up for ever.

From my first month I knew I was trapped in an
educational system for which I was never designed, based
on the requirements of industry and urban living. We
studied to pass exams, to pass other exams, to get safe
jobs, to live happily ever after in an urban paradise. That
was the philosophy conveyed by those teachers who
showed any concern for us at all. Sterile textbook days
were chipped away, exercise by exercise, stanza by stanza,
experiment after experiment, and homework was more of
the same. What could have been a joyous experience was
like climbing a pyramid only to find weeds growing at the
top and the treasure inside still unattainable. The school
library was contained in one glass-fronted bookcase, no
bigger than the one in our dining room at home; my own
library was bigger.

Amongst town pupils and the teachers there was a

scarcely veiled contempt for those of us who came from the country. We lived in hamlets without artificial light, piped water or shops. We were the ones who arrived at school wet, muddy and windswept, were booked for being late, and who handed in homework besmirched by rain. We were the 'weaklings' who, after seven o'clock breakfast and a cycle ride of five or six miles, stood in Assembly for half an hour and fainted. For six years I endured the system; endured the day but revelled in self-education at night. I successfully concealed my true identity from those who did not deserve to know — my masters, but not my betters. In term time I offered just enough to satisfy work norms; in exams I took my revenge by winning prizes for every subject in the curriculum. Not a teacher understood why and thereby they stand indicted.

IN THE 1920s few in our family dared to talk about careers for that would be to suppose that a choice existed. But times were hard and unemployment high so we were content to work, save, hope and keep an open mind as to how each of us would ultimately use our talents. However, Mother left me in no doubt that the better I performed at school the brighter my prospects, and this acted as a real spur. But little did the nine Cramp children who sat round the table in 1920 think that, by the end of the decade, only two would remain at home.

Almost, it seemed, we left home in age order. Robert left first in 1922 having saved enough capital to start farming on his own account. He was also lucky, for farms were to be had at give-away rents. Muriel left next to marry a farmer. For Eric and Douglas there was no hope of a farm. They had youth and strength, but no capital, so both decided to emigrate to New Zealand. I recall their separate departures. It was probably the only morning of their life since the age of thirteen, when they left school, that they hadn't milked a cow. Ironically, each began his journey across the world by riding to the station in the milkcart, cabin trunk standing upended amidst the milk churns. Neither was farm routine varied at their departure. Our man drove the horse and cart as usual, and no one shed a tear as they left.

In 1928 I entered the school Sixth Form, destined for a scholastic career; but for the next two years, until I entered University, life as an academic in a farmhouse was far from easy. Whenever I wished to apply myself to homework, there was always a farm job which Father would pointedly say could be much better done 'with another pair of hands'. In summertime it was, 'If only we had someone to get the cows in and start milking, we could stay longer in the hayfield.' Or again, 'Old So-and-so has let me down. I was relying on him. We need someone with experience.' But encouraged by Mother, I learned to harden my heart, shed any feelings of guilt, and make any help that I gave fit into my own programme.

The further I threw myself into studies, the more remote became the topics of domestic conversation. I could no longer care deeply about the cow that had milk fever after calving, the bullock that strayed into the next parish, the sheep that needed dipping, the calves that were scouring or the milk that was tainted with butter-cups. In my simple study bedroom, I would sometimes pause in the midst of Economics, History, Latin and other studies, and catch the sounds of farm routine. Occasionally, I would yearn for a life spent among the fields and woods of my boyhood, and wonder if my chosen path was right. But sanity would return when I remembered how little time farming left for cultural pursuits. One summer evening a bat flew into my room. I found it next day hanging from a book by W. Nevinson, called *More Changes, More Chances*. This omen was never forgotten, and I determined that one day I would have money and leisure enough to travel.

The manual labour I gave on the farm was good relaxation. But my best contribution to farm life after the age of sixteen was probably in the writing of business letters and, as farming became more sophisticated, in keeping records, completing Department of Agriculture returns, and preparing details for that newcomer to the farming scene, the Accountant. Father accepted new business methods with reluctance and was therefore difficult to help.

The following is typical of a conversation with Father, as I tried to bring some order into his book-keeping:

'How much did you sell the haystack for?'

'Well, I only sold half really.'

'To whom?'

'To the merchant, but he offset part of it against clover seed I bought.'

'Did you sow the seed?'

'No! In the finish I sold it to Mr Watts.'

'For how much?'

'He hasn't paid yet. You see I use his bull for my cows now and we settle up every year or so.'

'What happened to the other half of the haystack?'

'It's sort of offset. I let Robert (son) have it. He's going to help me in haytime. I'm also going to put fifty ewes in his big field rent free, but we're going to share the wool and the lambs.'

And so it went on, rather like a game of chess with move and counter move. Every time it seemed one had come to the end of a transaction, there arose from it another deal, a 'contra', an 'offset', a shared something or other, a loan of men or machines or horses. Father was always most reluctant to measure his deals, his assets, his profits and losses, in hard cash. He would, for instance, reluctantly agree that bullocks bought in the spring and grazed through to autumn and sold fat, had done 'pretty fair'. But since the money was quickly rolled over and used to buy lamb-hogs for wintering, he refused to think in terms of profit on the bullocks. He preferred always, as he put it, 'to count the number of legs and divide by four', meaning to think of his assets in growing numbers of cattle, sheep, cows and pigs, and in extra grazing land he had rented in addition to the main farm. As he again put it he was more interested in 'woolly backs' than 'green-backs' (pound notes), and in making sure he could carry on his way of life to the end of his days. He always maintained that what interest farmers used to have in money vanished when gold coins went out of circulation. At least a sovereign, like a bullock, had intrinsic value you could see. Even with sovereigns, he said he once knew a farmer who could only estimate his wealth by the bucketful. This man had inherited a large fortune from an uncle, and when informed by the bank, insisted on withdrawing it in gold. Satisfied when he saw it nearly filled a bucket, he returned it to the bank. Annually from that point, his accountant had to estimate his total assets in terms of bucketfuls of sovereigns. Father did not say what happened when England left the gold standard.

None in our family sought to take over the farm in Father's declining years. He himself did not expect us to do so nor did he press us. Our careers had been made elsewhere. In any case who can follow the master? Father adapted to circumstance and age. He sold the farm to a corporate Trust but to the end still farmed a few score acres in the Langtons. His daily work was his memorial.

As I look back over the ten years of my growing up from a child of eight in 1920, to the verge of manhood in 1930, I have thought often about the profits and losses of that decade. But always I conclude that life in a large family is so complex as to defy evaluation. I have slept three in a bed and worn hand-me-down clothes; risen hungry from table; conformed to please others; and often submerged my fears and tears, my hopes and even my laughter, for lack of someone who could appreciate me as self, instead of judging me as a member of a family. But I have also known companionship and adventure and the stimulation of the varied interests of farm-life. In my village, I have known men full of wisdom and seen old men die happy after uncomplicated lives. I have lived close to Nature, that great teacher and philosopher, and sometimes alone by stream and woodland, or even sitting at table with ten others, briefly put my hand into the hand of God. I have known hard work and discipline too, and borne responsibility beyond my years. But I have also gained a breadth and depth of experience, far outweighing that of any formal education, and in particular, a capacity to enjoy the simple things of life.

And I have the memories.